MODERN SCIENT

G000230064

A compilation of lectures provid
fresh and informative materia. ... .
advanced students of hypnotism.

By the same author

SELF-IMPROVEMENT THROUGH SELF-HYPNOSIS

MODERN SCIENTIFIC HYPNOSIS

From Ancient Mystery to Contemporary Science

by

R.N. SHROUT

THORSONS PUBLISHERS LIMITED
Wellingborough, Northamptonshire

First published 1985

British Library Cataloguing in Publication Data

Shrout, Richard N.
  Modern scientific hypnosis: from ancient
  mystery to contemporary science.
  1. Hypnotism
  I. Title
  154.7   BF11141

ISBN 0-7225-0988-X

Printed and bound in Great Britain

Contents

1.

Four Pathways to the Subconscious

I want to begin by talking about what I call the 'Four Pathways to the Subconscious'. I often give this material to clients as a 'preliminary session' before I ever proceed to hypnotize them. Those of you who are interested primarily in self-improvement and self-knowledge will find this section particularly important. Understanding these 'Four Pathways to the Subconscious' will help you to learn how your mind works, how the subconscious mind works in yourself and others, and how you can gain access to your subconscious.

Definition of the Subconscious

To begin with we must define the subconscious. This is not easy because there are many 'metaphysical' definitions and many people who think of the subconscious as a kind of spooky or non-material thing. I don't like to think of the subconscious in the same terms as 'soul' or 'spirit'. I believe in the soul and the spirit, but I do not talk about them when I am speaking about hypnosis because it seems to me to be inappropriate terminology.

The subconscious mind, as I understand it within the context of scientific hypnosis, is an organic and somewhat materialistic concept. We know that we not only have the brain and spinal cord as a control centre, but also we can basically divide our nervous system into two divisions. The central nervous system (brain and spinal nerves) controls voluntary action and the autonomic nervous system controls involuntary action. This autonomic nervous system is divided further into two parts: the sympathetic and parasympathetic systems. Our whole body (muscles and organs) reacts by means of the entire nervous system without much conscious thought. So my definition of the subconscious (within the context of hypnosis) is merely 'the sum total of all the neurological and biochemical functions of the organism which operate below the level of conscious awareness'.

Now, you may say that I have just explained it all away, but no, I just put it into perspective; I keep the subconscious within your nervous system and within the confines of your body. It is everything that takes place — the sum total of all the functions of your nervous system, the endocrine system, all the electrochemical functions of your body which take place below the level of your conscious awareness. That is what we mean by 'subconscious' — it merely means all that is going on *that you are not consciously aware of*. Having said that, however, I will probably lapse into talking about it as if it were a thing in itself, from lifelong habit.

Two Kinds of Reasoning

It is important to understand how your subconscious mind 'thinks'. (If it is part of your nervous system it is natural to speak of this as 'thinking'.) You read sometimes that the subconscious mind does not reason, but this is not altogether true. There are two kinds of reasoning and it is important that you know this in order to understand how the subconscious reasons.

The two kinds of reasoning are *inductive* and *deductive*. I'll try to explain it a bit. *Deductive reasoning* is when you begin with a generalization, theory, or premise, and you reason toward the specific. *Inductive reasoning* is when you begin with individual data and reason from that back to some kind of a theory. In other words, when Newton saw the apple fall from the tree, he saw an isolated phenomenon and began to reason about it to form a general theory. In effect, he reasoned inductively about everything else that fell down, gathering more data, and asked, 'What explains this?' Then he proposed the theory of gravity's force that pulls things down. This illustrates the process of inductive reasoning: gathering data and inducing a theory from which it would account for all the known facts.

In deductive reasoning, you take the theory that is propounded and you deduct from that theory. You say, 'Now if this theory is true, then under given circumstances this would be true, that would be true, and the other would be true.' (Or, if the theory be true, then under certain circumstances other things would *never* happen.) Then you test the theory.

This represents two kinds of reasoning: one is inductive, where you reason from a number of specific things to a generalized premise; the other is deductive, where you reason from the premise down to the specifics.

The Deductive Subconscious

Now, the way this works out as far as the subconscious is concerned is simply this: our conscious mind (the mind you are using to read and analyse right now) reasons in *both* of these ways. All of us can and do reason both inductively and deductively. However, the subconscious mind (or the kind of thinking that you do when you are in what we call a hypnotic state) is that state of mind which *only* reasons deductively. Therefore you can say *the subconscious mind cannot reason inductively; it only reasons deductively.* You may say, 'Well, what does that mean?' It means, for example, if I say to you now, 'The room is getting colder. This room is getting colder and colder. You can feel it getting colder' and you think about it awhile and say, 'Now wait a minute. I don't feel it getting colder. What is this, some kind of a trick he's playing? It's not really getting colder, is it? Does anyone else feel it's getting colder? Maybe it's colder where he is standing. Maybe he's getting a chill and perhaps that's why he said that. Let's just look at the thermometer and see if it is really getting colder.' That is inductive reasoning. You think, 'Let's examine the data and see if it supports this theory that the room is getting colder.'

However, *if in a state of hypnosis* we tell your subconscious mind the *very same thing*, namely, 'The room is getting colder. It is getting colder and colder. You can feel it getting colder.' something altogether different takes place because your subconscious mind *accepts my premise* that the room is getting colder. That is a fact *as far as the subconscious mind is concerned.* The subconscious does not have the ability to question the validity of that statement — it may not accept it fully but it is not going to reason inductively about it; it is accepted either totally or partially. It does not look for independent evidence. The subconscious mind accepts the idea that, 'the room is getting colder', and then, *that being accepted as true,* everything which would logically follow deductively from that premise would also be true, and you would begin to feel colder. Your whole being will react psychologically and physiologically as if in a cold room. You will feel colder, you will act as if you were colder, and all the rest of us who are not in that hypnotic state of mind (who are still reasoning inductively) look at you shivering and exclaim, 'Goodness, isn't this interesting?'

What is happening is that your critical faculty has been temporarily by-passed or suspended so you can *only* reason in a deductive way. From studies in hypnosis, we can assert that the subconscious mind reasons by deduction only and never by inductive reasoning. That's why the subconscious mind is capable of believing many, many things which *are not necessarily true at all*!

The Off-Conscious State

Now, to simplify this (and we have to over-simplify a subject as complex as this), let's just think of the conscious and subconscious minds as two ends of the same stick: all *one mind*, but still *two functions* and *two ways* of operating. The two aspects of the mind are in *constant relative balance* one with the other, like a child's see-saw. By that I mean when one is 'up' (so to speak) or one end is in control, the other is 'down'. Both ends cannot be 'up' at the same time. When you are in a fully conscious state throughout the day, your conscious mind is on top. When you go to sleep, nature has a way of closing off the subconscious mind as a protective device, to prevent anyone with an evil intent from influencing your subconscious mind while you sleep. So, when you sleep, nature steps in and 'shuts the door' to your subconscious mind. However, there are times in our experience when we get a little bit 'off-conscious' for one reason or another, and our conscious mind can be pictured as being 'down' a little, with the result that the subconscious emerges or is 'up' a little. Then, whatever we or others say can affect the subconscious mind.

The Computer Analogy

Let's continue to over-simplify this concept and use the 'cybernetic' or 'computer' approach to understand the subconscious mind. I think it's very helpful to look at your subconscious as a mechanism, like a computer. Now, a computer is only as good as the information which is programmed into it. There are fantastic computers used in space programmes which can figure out intricate orbits, the fuel consumption to the moon and back, etc., but I am sure those same computers could not tell you the capital of France if you asked! Why not? Because computers do only what they are programmed to do. The subconscious mind is like a computer and it is also programmed. Therefore, when I speak of the 'Four Pathways to the Subconscious', I am talking about four ways in which the subconscious mind is programmed.

I think it is important to accept this concept because *everyone's subconscious mind is normal*, in the sense that it does exactly what it was created to do. A person may have very abnormal behaviour and very bizarre ideas, but there is nothing wrong with the mechanisms of the subconscious. Their subconscious mind is doing exactly what it is meant to do — it is being programmed, and based upon the input it gives an output. There is a saying in the computer business, 'rubbish in, rubbish out'. That means no matter how magnificent the computer is, it must be programmed properly. So, the subconscious mind is like a computer and we are all programmed subconsciously for health, happiness, success, etc., or we can be programmed for sickness, pessimism, unhappiness, or failure. Yet our subconscious mind in either case is simply doing what it is supposed to do, it is *acting deductively on the basis of what has been programmed into it*.

Now let us consider the four ways by which the subconscious mind is programmed.

THE FIRST PATHWAY: CHILDHOOD PROGRAMMING

The first way that the subconscious is programmed is in early childhood. People often ask whether it is possible to hypnotize a very young child. Usually you read that you cannot hypnotize anyone under the age of six or some arbitrary number like that. I suppose this is true if you consider hypnosis only in the classical sense of formal inductions. However, you do not have to hypnotize very young children because, in a real sense, they are already hypnotized. They are in a 'trance state' *in the sense that they have not yet developed a true ability to reason inductively.* A child under four or five years of age cannot reason inductively; its critical faculty has not yet developed. That's why a child learns by suggestion and by imitation, and it is only around five or six years that it begins to reason in the inductive mode.

Santa Claus Logic

A very good example of this fact is that millions of children believe in Santa Claus. How many of you believed in Santa Claus? I did, and I think if the truth were known, almost all of us did at an early period of life. Now, let us analyse this story we so firmly believed in. There is a man who lives at the North Pole (and if you can believe *that*, you obviously aren't reasoning inductively). This man potters around all year making toys and one night out of the year he takes these toys to the good little girls and boys, and he knows which are the good ones and which aren't, because you cannot fool good old Santa. So, one night out of the whole year, this man who lives at the North Pole flies through the air in a sleigh, and goes down the chimneys and takes toys to the good little girls and boys, through the whole town, and all over the world, in one night! Now, we could sit all night pooling our collective mental resources and we could not come up with a more absurd, illogical, crazy, nonsensical story than that — and yet we believed it! We even believed it so passionately that when some older child said, 'There isn't any Santa Claus', we declared, 'Yes there is. I know there is'. I asked how we know this was so we would reply, 'Well, I know because my mother said so, that's why!'

That settled it for us at that age and it is easy to see what we mean when we say that a young child does not reason inductively. He does not have the ability at an early age to reason inductively; this is something that comes with maturation. Now, the point is, our parents told us many things when we were small and which were not any more true than Santa Claus, and this is where you get into the bad programming which goes into the subconscious mind of a child.

Positive and Negative Programming

So, whatever is said to a child — whatever was *said* to us, whatever *happened* to us in those first five or six years — gives the *initial programming* to the subconscious. If it was positive input, then it was positive programming; if it was negative input, then we received some negative programming. So what we say to a child or what was said to you as a child, has the same effect on the subconscious mind as would a hypnotic suggestion given to a hypnotized adult.

Are you aware of what people say to children? You hear them say negative things to children in stores, shopping centres, everywhere. Perhaps you can remember the negative things you heard as a child. You may recall with chagrin having said negative things to your own or others' children. Think of it as if they were hypnotic suggestions given to you now, as an adult, and you will see the importance of it, negative statements like this: 'You stupid thing. Can't you ever learn? Won't you ever get anything right'? 'You be quiet. Nobody wants to listen to you.' 'Shame on you. That's dirty, filthy, nasty and you ought to be ashamed of yourself!'

All of this is programmed automatically into a child's innocent and defenceless mind which has not yet developed a critical faculty. So, we wonder why it is when ten, twenty, thirty, forty or fifty years later we have all sorts of odd little 'hang-ups'.

Mental Blocks

We wonder why we cannot learn certain things, or why we *think* we cannot learn certain things, and we have these *self-imposed* 'mental blocks'. We moan, 'I'd better not take a class in that course. That's too hard. I'm not very good at that'. Now, where did we get that kind of thinking? Why do we think, 'Oh, literature is easy, but maths are hard. Spanish is easy, but Russian or Chinese is hard', etc.? If we took the phrase 'Mary had a little lamb' and just wrote it phonetically in the Russian alphabet (or any foreign language which does not use our alphabet) and said, 'Now class, let's have a language lesson today. Here it is', many would think, 'Oh my God, I can't learn *that!*' Why do you think it's harder to learn Chinese than Spanish? There are more people who speak Chinese than speak Spanish, and they are not so smart. Why do we have those ideas? It is important to think these things through, because people are always saying, 'I can't learn this or that'.

However, if we consider the smartest professor in the world, we will realize that the only reason he is smarter than us is because he learned something we didn't, and he learned it from someone else. Furthermore, logic tells us that anything that can be learned can be taught, and if it can be taught, then you can learn it. There is no question about it, except that you subconsciously had it programmed into you that you cannot learn or do certain things. ('You stupid thing, can't you ever learn, can't you do anything right?') You simply have this defeatist programming from an early age.

This is also why there is a widespread fear of public speaking in many people. They cannot even speak up in a small group and express themselves. Why is this? The adult mind says, 'Wait a minute. I'm just as good as these people', (or a really negative thinker might think, 'They're just as bad as I am') but either way you know you are equal to them. But your 'little child mind' (like an echo from the subconscious) is saying, 'You be quiet. Nobody wants to listen to you'.

Many people have guilt feelings which they should not have. (I am different from many people in that I believe there *are* valid guilt feelings, and a lot of people *should* feel a lot guiltier than they do.) The people who have guilt complexes are usually very conscientious and compulsive. You see, guilt is abnormal only if it is out of proportion to what caused it. For example, the man who is ready to jump off a bridge, because in 1968 he stole a postage stamp from an employer and he can't stand the guilt, would certainly need help! This is silly neurotic guilt. But a person who feels guilty 'without a reason' really does have a reason — a subconscious reason — which is the result of some kind of subconscious programming that tells him, 'You ought to feel ashamed of yourself'. Even when he is not ashamed of himself, he feels guilty because he feels he *ought* to be ashamed of himself! It's a vicious circle, a 'double-bind', a damned-if-you-do and damned-if-you-don't situation. There is no escape from the effects of this kind of programming from early childhood.

Now, I have just given you negative examples and it is not all negative. People can say positive things to a child like, 'Oh, did you draw that? That's very good. You can draw really well'. If that happened to you in nursery school, you probably ran home with your built-up little ego and shouted, 'Mum, my teacher said today that I drew really well!' So, our subconscious programming in childhood has to be fifty-one per cent positive, for otherwise we would never survive at all. However, the point is that the first five or six years of our lives are crucial, because it is then that we get the initial programming of our subconscious. This is agreed upon by all psychologists and psychiatrists, whatever their theoretical framework, but I have given you the *hypnological interpretation* of this. The early years are important because it is the time when the initial programming takes place.

From that age on, we soon developed a *critical faculty*, that is, we began to develop the ability to reason inductively. This happened, in part, very simply because people began to lie to us and cheat and take advantage of us, so we learned that not everyone can be taken at face value. Therefore little children reach the age when they say, 'The child down the street said so-and-so, but I don't believe him'.

The Critical Faculty

The development of a critical faculty was the beginning of our ability to reason inductively, and from that time in our development the subconscious mind is programmed in other ways. After we have the ability to reason both inductively and deductively, we use this critical faculty to *analyse*, to *filter thoughts*, and to *learn* from the experience of others as well as our own, from books, libraries, history, etc. But how is the subconscious mind programmed after we develop this critical faculty?

THE SECOND PATHWAY: TRAUMA

The second pathway to the subconscious is through what are called 'traumatic experiences'. The word 'traumatic' means, 'a wound or injury; a disordered state resulting from emotional stress or physical injury; an agent, force, or mechanism that causes such damage'. It has either a physical or psychological meaning. If you break a leg, you can say your leg suffers a severe trauma. However, here we are talking about *psychologically damaging experiences*. Psychiatrists can often trace a neurosis or problem to an earlier event which they call a 'traumatic experience'. It was the original 'psychic fracture' from which the problem began and which later grew and developed into a full-blown problem, perhaps many years later. These traumatic experiences are those experiences which are emotionally damaging, and I want to explain from a hypnological point of view just why and how they programme your subconscious mind.

I explained earlier about the see-saw model of the mind and what is meant by an 'off-conscious' state. Whenever you are under the influence of a strong emotion, you are (to that extent) a little bit 'off-conscious'. The key phrase here is 'under the influence of', for it is like being 'under the influence' of alcohol; whenever you are under the influence of a strong emotion your mind *is* slightly 'off-conscious'. You are not unconscious, but you are definitely off-conscious. This emotion may be positive or negative, it makes no difference. In the nature of things, however, the emotional context preceding most traumatic experiences is negative. For example, when you are afraid or fearful ('full of fear'), paralysed with fear, etc., you are 'off-conscious'. You are not thinking straight if you are enraged or angry to the point where you can hardly see clearly, or you are hardly able to talk and you are losing more control every second — then you are 'off-conscious'. If you are so bereaved and grief-stricken that you can only sit feeling totally deprived and bereft and numb, you are 'off-conscious'. In such 'off-conscious' states, anything you hear, anything said to you, anything you read, or any idea that would spontaneously 'pop into your mind', all will have the force of a hypnotic suggestion because they influence and program your subconscious mind.

Any time you are under the influence of a strong emotion to the point that if someone suddenly asked your name, you would have to stop and think for a while, you are obviously 'off-conscious'. Whenever you are not in control of your own mind due to a strong emotion, you are 'off-conscious' (the subconscious end of the see-saw is 'up') and anything which enters your mind then can have *all the force of a hypnotic suggestion*!

Perception Versus Experience

In a traumatic experience, the *experience itself* is not really the important thing. The important thing is how you *reacted* to it, how you *perceived* it, and what it *meant* to you at the time.

You can find people who have been through a war, perhaps they were in a prisoner-of-war camp, perhaps tortured, witnessing terrible atrocities, all most traumatic experiences. But when they come home they say, 'Oh, I'm glad to be back. I'm lucky to be back', and they are fully functioning, doing quite well — they're not all that emotionally or psychologically torn up. They went through those horrible experiences but it did not seem to be traumatic to them on a *subconscious* level!

On the other hand, you find the streets are full of emotionally crippled people who cannot even function due to some small thing that did not really amount to much, but has so affected them that it hindered their adjustment and development throughout their entire adult life. Now what's the difference?

You can go past a school playground and find a small child screaming his head off as the teacher and bigger children try to restrain this little monster who is turning purple with rage and screaming, 'Let me loose, I'll kill him, I'll kill him!' Why all this fuss? 'Well, he made me drop my lollipop; I'll kill him!'

To the child, losing that lollipop is more traumatic than for a soldier who has his leg blown off, because only one of them is perceiving the event as a damaging end-of-the-world sort of experience. It is not the nature of what actually happens that makes a traumatic experience, but the perception of it. This is why people can be trapped in a coal mine or in a submarine and they do not necessarily develop claustrophobia. But if you take a small child and lock him in a cupboard, or if you are a teenager and while fooling around get locked in a car boot so that you cannot get out when you thought you could, these can be traumatic claustrophobia-producing experiences. If you become paralysed by fear, you are in an 'off-conscious' state in which ideas may penetrate the subconscious mind and create serious problems later on. There are so many ways in which this kind of thing can happen.

There are people who are convinced that they have some incurable disease simply because they had a medical examination while feeling so apprehensive that they were slightly 'off-conscious' and they overheard a remark not intended for them (that perhaps referred to someone else's tests) which influenced the subconscious. They were not consciously aware of even receiving the idea because they were so frightened at the time that the impression was completely subconscious.

Whenever you are under the influence of a strong emotion (such as during a traumatic experience) you become 'off-conscious', exposing your subconscious mind to random impressions which take on hypnotic force. Thus, the traumatic experiences of life program the subconscious.

THE THIRD PATHWAY: AUTOSUGGESTION

The third pathway to the subconscious, the third way it is programmed, is through autosuggestion. Now, autosuggestion has to do with *how we habitually think*. People often think that autosuggestion means that you carry a little card in your purse or pocket which has a snappy little 'affirmation' written on it, and you take it out and read it a few times a day. That is a pretty narrow view of what it means to suggest things to yourself. Autosuggestion refers to the way you habitually think because when you think you *talk to yourself mentally.* You cannot think without talking to yourself mentally. So autosuggestion is not really a matter of reading or just saying things to yourself, but of *thinking* them. Actually saying them is to force you to think about them.

Your Inner Voice

The point is this: you may not believe what *other* people tell you, but you *always tend to believe what you tell yourself*! For example, someone can insult you and call you all kinds of obscene names, they can be just as belligerent and hostile as you can imagine — but *if* you are really in control of your mind it does not affect your subconscious. It might bother you, but it would not actually harm you. You know there is nothing wrong with you, so it must be him! (After all, if he really knew what a wonderful person you are, he'd be nice and maybe even offer to buy you a drink.)

If you are in *full control*, your critical faculty filters out all those insults. But then you get rid of that person and start to think over the conversation. This is where trouble really begins.

You begin to think along these lines, 'Wait a minute. Come to think of it, he may be right. I haven't been doing very well lately and I've made a lot of mistakes recently and perhaps I'm not a very good person. Maybe he was just telling me the truth. Perhaps he is the only honest person I've met; maybe everyone thinks of me that way and just won't tell me to spare my feelings. The reason this person said those things is because they are the truth'. After brooding like that, you have *talked yourself* right down into the dumps. You get depressed and then angry. You snap out of it and mutter, 'That person! I wish I hadn't met him. He ruined my day!' He didn't ruin it, you did! A hundred people like him could not have ruined it until you began to accept what he was saying, *then* it affected you. That is because autosuggestion has to do with the way *you* think, for when you think, you are talking to yourself mentally.

Positive Thinking

Now you can see the importance of positive thinking. You can see the devastating effects of negative thinking, because a person who goes around thinking negatively all the time is programming his subconscious with negative autosuggestions. The person who *habitually* thinks positively and optimistically is *constantly* programming his subconscious mind in a positive way. This is what positive and negative thinking is all about.

It is so important to understand this, because people always expect somebody else to do the work that only *they* can do with their own minds. They want to pay a doctor to *make* them well, to pay a teacher to *make* them clever, and want to go to church to *make* them good, or whatever. It doesn't work that way. People have to help themselves, and unless a person's own thinking becomes habitually changed there is not going to be any lasting change.

I tell the people who come to me for clinical hypnosis that they can go out of my office feeling like a million dollars, but if they begin to think in their old negative, defeatist way again before they have driven half-way home it's all going to wear off. It will be a piecemeal kind of therapy that wears off before they get home with it, because they themselves have undone it.

Dedicated to Defeat

Now, there *is* great power in hypnosis because there is great power in the subconscious mind, but if I saw you one hour every day of your life, you still have twenty-three hours each day to undo what I can do in one hour! Therefore, one good 'dedicated' negative thinker can undo what a hundred hypnotherapists could do for him. All we can do is give the initial positive programming, but if people do not learn to think habitually in a more positive way and develop the habit and attitude of positive thinking, then it is not going to do them all that much good; it will be very temporary indeed.

Autosuggestion has to do with the way you think all the time. If you want to be well and happy and prosperous, then get your mind *off* what you *don't* want and *on* to the things you *do* want, for that's the only way it can happen.

THE FOURTH PATHWAY: HYPNOSIS

The fourth pathway to the subconscious mind is through hypnosis. Now, hypnosis just does what all these other 'pathways to the subconscious' do — it gets your mind into an 'off-conscious' state so that what is said registers on the subconscious. The only artificial thing about it is that you choose the time, the place and the purpose for which you induce this 'off-conscious' state. There is nothing artificial about the state of hypnosis, for you have been in that state of mind many times in your life.

Twice-Daily Trances

Actually, you've been in hypnosis twice a day every day of your life. *Everybody has been in a hypnotic trance twice a day*! All of your life, every night as you go to sleep, you do not go to sleep instantly. You 'fall' asleep gradually. You just close your eyes and lie there and soon your hearing fades out and you are asleep. When you wake up in the morning, it is all in reverse: first you hear, then you open your eyes and begin to move. Hypnosis is a kind of 'transitional' sleep. It is just in-between 'sound asleep' and 'wide awake'. It is a hypnotic state because it is an 'off-conscious' state of mind where you are conscious but not fully conscious; you're asleep but you're not fully asleep.

Negative Trance

How do we get this 'off-conscious' state in hypnosis? Well, we could do it the way traumatic experience does it, that is, we could stimulate your emotions. We could scare you out of your wits and that would create an 'off-conscious' state that would be a hypnotic trance — an unpleasant one to be sure, but a hypnotic trance nonetheless. That was what Mesmer and Charcot did, and what stage hypnotists still do to an extent — there is a frightening, intimidating element involved. For example, if I used an authoritarian technique to hypnotize you, you would get the feeling that I am symbolic of all the authority figures you have ever known, and you are just a poor, helpless, defenceless little thing. This would bring on the kind of negative hypnotic trance which can be induced by stimulating a negative emotion. It is like a miniature traumatic experience. Obviously, we do not do things that way very much in modern clinical hypnosis practice.

Positive Trace

Then how do we get you in an 'off-conscious' state? We do it simply by *relaxation*. We literally relax you into it and, as you relax, your *conscious* mind relaxes. It does not go to sleep, because if you went to sleep then nature would step in and close that door to the subconscious. The conscious mind does not go to sleep in hypnosis, but we can say that the *resistance* of the conscious mind goes to sleep. The critical faculties get by-passed as the conscious mind sinks down into a lazy, drowsy state of semi-lethargy where it just could not care less what is going on.

Perhaps you have been in this state of mind when you were bored stiff at a party or gathering of some kind. You are in a corner, bored with the whole thing, and you could easily go to sleep. It is getting late and you are waiting for someone, and you hear people laughing and talking in your 'off-conscious' state. You think, 'I know who that is; he's always laughing at some stupid thing . . .' but you don't care what it is all about. The conscious mind is beginning to relax and so creates a hypnotic possibility, if you could only control it. If you could control the relaxation, you would be able to experience the effortless concentration of hypnosis.

Effortless Concentration

Some people are interested in hypnosis for the possibility of better learning, concentration, memory, etc. The way this works must be effortless, for concentration should be effortless; if it is not, it is not effective concentration. Really effective concentration is always done without effort.

Suppose you come up to someone who is working something out and they are frowning and squinting, biting their lips, etc. You speak to them and they jump because you startle them. 'Good grief!', they complain, 'Can't you see I'm concentrating?' No, they are not. They are only *trying hard* to concentrate, but they are not doing it. If they were, they would just be effortlessly absorbed in what they are doing. You would come up and stand on one foot and then the other, you would cough until you had finally intruded on their awareness. They would turn and deal with you, dismiss you from their mind and go right back to what they were doing, effortlessly absorbed in it. Now, this is concentration!

When you ask people to concentrate on something, they always try to make a physical activity out of it. You could say, 'Concentrate on that picture on the wall. Look at it and concentrate on it. Concentrate very hard on it.' They would probably hunch their shoulders and squint a little, thinking they were concentrating 'hard'. After a while, they would say, 'Wow! I'm getting a stiff neck and a headache. That concentrating really is hard work!' Well, you see, if you make a physical activity out of it, then it has got to be hard, but *concentration is not a physical activity — it is a mental activity.*

When we are really concentrating, we are completely relaxed and oblivious to everything else, including our own body, our physical position, and so on. Therefore, in hypnosis (when we get a person in a completely relaxed state) there is no anxiety, there is no tension, and then you have the possibility of *effortless* concentration.

Awareness

You have experienced this feeling many times. Let me illustrate it this way: your awareness at any given moment can be illustrated as concentric circles. In the inner circle right now, for example, (if you are paying attention) your inner circle contains what I am saying to you as you think about the meaning of it. Maybe you are formulating questions, or analysing and comparing ideas, etc.

Beyond that, in the next circle, *at the very same time*, you are aware of other people who might be in the room, you are aware of where you are, etc. In the next circle, you are aware of your family and friends; in the next circle is your awareness of your job, etc. Beyond that in another circle you are aware of current events and the political situation. Beyond that is another circle of awareness that contains the name of your first primary school teacher, etc. It is all 'in there', but some of it seems 'out there' because your awareness is like concentric circles. If I say, 'Tell me about your senior school', or, 'Tell me about your family', it is no effort for you to *shift the focus* of your attention. But when you do, that becomes your 'inner circle', and all the other contents in your general awareness automatically are rearranged in other concentric circles around your focal point. The position of things in your general awareness can always be imagined in concentric circles which are relative to the inner circle, which is your focus of attention at any given moment.

Shifting Awareness

To give another example of what happens when you shift your awareness to another focal point, consider the following situation: perhaps you have been in a restaurant with a companion when you heard someone laughing or talking from a table across the room. For some reason, you become interested in what they are talking about. Your attention is attracted and you begin to concentrate on that conversation. You begin to narrow your awareness, shifting it over to them, *away from* the person who is sitting opposite you. As you shift your awareness and listen to the other conversation, it seems after a while as if all the noises in the restaurant are far away, becoming blurred and indistinct. While you are concentrating on that person over there it seems as if (I am sure it is mostly an illusion) you are almost 'tuned in' to the point when you can almost understand what they are talking about. About the time you think you've 'got it', the person across your table says something to you and you respond, 'Sorry?' *You missed it completely!* This is what I mean by how, in your awareness, everything is in a changing relationship to something else.

Restricting Awareness

In hypnosis, through the process of complete relaxation, what we do is *narrow down* the awareness; we *restrict* the awareness. Now, you can do this by staring at a light, and if you continue long enough, you've *got* to restrict your awareness. What can you be aware of, except the light? There are many, many other ways of doing it, but no matter how we do it, we have to restrict this general awareness — we have to push it all in, bring it inward from the outer circles, compress all the power and awareness of your mind together and focus it *on one thing only*. In that case, it would be the words the hypnotist is saying *at that given moment*.

That is why you lose all sense of time or space, or bodily awareness. When you have this *positive trance* induced by relaxation, restricted awareness, and effortless concentration, there is a certain change in your bodily sensations. This is a neurological alteration which necessarily has to take place as you move into this 'off-conscious' state of mind where the subconscious mind is amenable to verbal suggestions. That is why we say a hypnotic trance makes you *hypersuggestible*, or more suggestible than usual.

2.

The History of Hypnosis

It seems necessary to discuss the history of hypnotism because one of the best ways to understand it is in its historical context. If we really want to comprehend any teaching, we ought to know the time and place from whence it came. We must keep in mind that various teachings were also recorded by a person who was a product of the educational and scientific system of his day. If we begin our study of hypnotism's modern scientific period, we have to begin with the Mesmer period, named after Franz Anton Mesmer, from 1760 to 1842. That, however, was not the real beginning of the phenomenon called hypnotism. The word 'hypnotism' did not exist until the mid-1800s, but its phenomena have existed long before then.

The Pre-Mesmer Period

Hypnotism was depicted in the works of antiquity by drawings on the caves and pottery etc., of the Egyptians and Assyrians. Many ancient cultures had drawings which apparently illustrate people being hypnotized: doctors setting bones, pulling teeth and so on, but with hocus-pocus gestures, such as little rays shooting out from the eyes or fingers, for instance. It is as if the stereotype of the stage hypnotist were represented in these ancient drawings and carvings.

It is sometimes cited as proof of the early use of hypnotism that brain operations and various other surgical operations were performed on people of ancient cultures. From fossils and mummies, experts can tell that there were successful brain operations because it is obvious that the people healed up and lived many years afterward. Since people survived these operations, it is presumed that some sort of hypnotic anaesthesia was used along with the surgical techniques. I do not completely agree with this. In Biblical times, warm wine was mixed with opium for anaesthetic purposes and major operations were performed with relative success. It is conceivable that primitive people also knew something about natural pain-killing drugs. I am not sure that those early drawings conclusively prove the use of hypnotism, but it does look that way.

Jewish and Greek Cultures

The compilation of ancient Hebrew wisdom known as the Talmud speaks of animal hypnotism at some length, saying it was permitted to charm poisonous serpents on the Sabbath. Thus by stretching the imagination a bit, we can say that 'hypnotism' is mentioned in the Talmud.

The ancient Greeks also had a form of hypnotism in their 'sleep temples'. The idea of the 'sleep temple' was prevalent in ancient Greece and Egypt. It probably started in Greece and through the Hellenic expansion it spread to Egypt as well.

Sophrology

In South America today, medical hypnosis is often known as 'Sophrology'. Some physicians have got away from the word 'hypnotism' altogether. They have taken a word from classical Greek medicine because the Greeks had a goddess named Sophresene, and people came to the temples of Sophresene (so the story goes) and were put into a sleep-like trance, listened to the 'beautiful discourse' of the priests of Sophresene, were healed and went about their daily chores 'happily ever after'. A psychiatrist in Barcelona studied ancient Greek medicine thoroughly and coined the term 'Sophrology' from the root 'sos', meaning 'tranquil', 'phren', meaning 'mind' (as in phrenology), and 'ology', meaning 'science' or 'the study of'.

Thus it is that many modern medical men in the Spanish-speaking world do not talk about 'hypnotism' because a hypnotist would therefore mean someone who literally puts people to 'sleep', which he really does not do. On the other hand, a 'sophrologist' would be one who 'treats the mind by making it tranquil', which is a much better concept and explanation of what really happens.

The whole point is that this new word which was coined, and is widely used in the Spanish-speaking world, was derived from the study of ancient Greek medicine and the practice of the priests of Sophresene. We can assume that the equivalents of hypnotism go back a long, long time — probably to the very beginning. The human mind being what it is, the practice of hypnotism had to evolve sooner or later.

The Mesmer Period

What we consider as the modern era of hypnotism began with the Mesmer period, from 1760 to 1842. Franz Anton Mesmer was a physician in Vienna and later in Paris. I want to emphasize that he was a scientist and an honest man. In fact, all the men we will study here were honourable men, although some of them have been very much maligned by historians. Mesmer was not a charlatan; his was not a scheme for seducing wealthy women, or any such thing. Mesmer was an honest, educated man. He represented the very best of the culture of his time.

There were interesting forces at work which led Mesmer to his theory of 'animal magnetism'. When he was a young lad, he happened to come across a woodcutter who had been injured by a falling tree. The man's leg was bleeding profusely. As Mesmer approached, he noticed that the man's wound stopped bleeding. As Mesmer turned away, he noticed it started bleeding again. He tentatively stretched out his hand over the wound, and it stopped bleeding; when he stepped back, it would bleed again! We know modern dentists who use hypnosis to control bleeding, so it is not as mysterious to us today as it must have seemed back then. You can imagine the impression it made on Mesmer! It started him thinking about his 'healing power', and he decided to become a physician.

Magnetism

One day as Mesmer walked down the street, he saw a sideshow going on. A conjurer had some people he had selected from the audience up on a little platform, and with a 'magnetized wand' he was demonstrating lodestones, or magnets, which were the rage of the scientific world in the mid-1700s. The man dramatically announced, 'We know that everything in nature is full of magnetism. Everything, minerals, plants, animals, and every created thing has magnetism. Now, the magnetism in this man's body is such that when I touch him with this magnetic wand he will cry and sob uncontrollably until I touch him again with the wand.' He touched the man, who starting sobbing as predicted. The conjurer went to the next person and said, 'Now, the magnetism in this man's body is such that when I touch him with the wand, he'll break into uncontrollable laughter until I restore him to normality with a second touch of the wand'. This also happened as predicted.

This was quite a show! When Mesmer walked away, he thought, 'If it's true that magnetism is in everything and everybody, this man has discovered something which could be of medical importance!' The whole premise was wrong but it was the beginning of his theory, which laid the foundations for hypnotism.

Father Hell and Father Gasner

Mesmer later learned of a famous astronomer and Jesuit priest, Father Maximillian Hell, who was a professor at the University of Vienna. Father Hell (1720-1792) had great success in curing people by placing magnets on them. He had magnets shaped like different organs of the body (heart, liver, kidney, etc.) and he would place them over a sick person's afflicted area. The fact that these magnets were so shaped makes me suspect that he knew his cures were as psychological as magnetic. If the curative power was really magnetic, the shape would make no difference. On the other hand, if he realized that the cures were psychological, then the shape of the magnets would have to appeal to the imagination. It sounds pretty primitive but this kind of thinking (the belief in talismans or amulets) has always been with us.

Whatever Father Hell did, he was successful at it. He achieved a cure rate of sixty-five to seventy per cent — any modern psychiatrist would be glad with that. Mesmer was fascinated with Hell's use of magnets in treating illness; it fitted his own theory of animal magnetism. (I used to tell a joke to the effect that Father Maximillian Hell built up his practice because many Viennese doctors got so exasperated with their neurotic patients they told them to 'go to hell!' The dismayed patients thought it over and decided he was referring them to Father Hell! In English, Hell sounds like an odd name for a priest. I soon discovered that in German, 'hell' means 'light' — an interesting name for an astronomer! 'Freud' in German means 'joy', and 'jung' means 'young'. It is fascinating to realize that Sigmund Freud's theories centred on the 'pleasure principle', and Carl Jung's theories prominently featured the idea of 're-birth'. There are many examples of names which are characteristic of either a person's physique or occupation, and some are quite humorous.

If this is not an example of the suggestive influence of a name, it certainly presents us with a novel coincidence.)

Mesmer was influenced also by another healer-priest. Father Gasner (1727-1779) was a very dramatic individual who spiced up his healing meetings with many theatricals. With flowing red robes, speaking Latin, he would touch patients with a large jewelled crucifix and they would fall down as though dead. He then 'cast out the demons', and restored them to 'a new life' by another touch of the huge metal crucifix. Father Gasner also had an impressive cure rate. Mesmer thought that the cures were 'magnetic' rather than religious. He reasoned that the crucifix was, in effect, a magnetic wand. He 'secularized' it by removing the cross-bar, and used such a wand in many of his own healing practices. He developed his theory of 'animal magnetism' and a method of therapy based on it, which later was derided as 'Mesmerism'.

Mesmer's Technique

The interesting thing about Mesmerism was that it often resulted in what we would call today convulsive trances. People went into convulsions, then catalepsy; some would faint dead away, and others would cry and moan. A few remained calm but most went into this 'crisis', as he called it. Mesmer believed that it was a healthy experience for patients to have this crisis of convulsions, where they might lie rigid for two or three hours at a time.

Mesmer developed the following method of treatment: he would sit across from a person and hold their thumbs, while 'explaining' how this altered the flow of magnetism from his body to theirs, and so on. Then he would begin to make 'passes', or downward motions of his hands. He would start at the head, not touching the person but keeping his hands a few inches from the skin, and make these 'magnetic passes' all the way down the body, implying that this altered the magnetic flow. He would go through this again and again, and perhaps for an hour or longer. Eventually the person would become 'magnetized' and begin to exhibit certain phenomena. Many who had convulsive experiences would come out of them feeling better or even claiming to be completely healed.

Mesmer wrote his doctoral dissertation on the theory of animal magnetism. Just as mineral magnetism has a force of attraction and repulsion, likewise in animals and humans there was a power which could be controlled. The reason a person was sick, he claimed, was because the magnetism of the body was 'out of sync', polarity-wise, and all you had to do was get it back in shape by restoring a harmonious flow once more.

The Baquet Seance

With all of Mesmer's practices, there was the idea that the power to heal resided in the person of the 'magnetizer'. Mesmer supposed this power emanated from his own body. But he soon conceived the idea of treating many people at the same time by constructing a big tub ('baquet' in French) filled with metal filings which were 'magnetized' by waving his hand over it. Glass rods were stuck into this at angles. People would sit around the tub, holding the glass rods and touching the person next to them. This was the healing seance. ('Seance' is just a French word meaning 'sitting'. There was absolutely no spiritualistic implication in Mesmer's work.)

People sat in a semi-darkened room absorbing all this 'magnetism' from the pile of filings in the tub. At a strategic moment, Mesmer would make his 'grand entrance' dressed in a flowing robe. He would go from person to person making a few passes, and they would go off into a cataleptic trance. Many were actually cured, a fact that we must keep in mind.

Today we know quite a lot about psychosomatic illnesses and hysterical illnesses, but no one knew this in Mesmer's time. All they knew was that people were cured. So many patients were trying to see him that Mesmer decided to train assistants. He even decided that his clients did not really have to see him or another magnetizer at all — all they needed to do was touch something which he had magnetized.

Mesmer solemnly 'magnetized' a tree in his garden. Then people came and touched the tree, and went into a trance with the same result as before. You can imagine how Mesmer's reputation grew as other doctors reported these happenings. Mesmer's activities were rather 'mind-bending' for the doctors of his day.

The Royal Commission

Mesmer's fame spread throughout Europe and into Russia and soon attracted so much attention that the King of France appointed a Royal Commission to study Mesmerism and decide what it was all about. This Royal Commission was formed from the greatest French scientists of the day. Benjamin Franklin, who had an international reputation as a scientist and inventor, was invited to participate in the investigations of the Royal Commission because he was serving as America's ambassador to France. The Commission observed some 'baquet seances' (a few were in Franklin's home in deference to his advanced age) which were conducted by a student of Mesmer's, Charles Deslon, while Mesmer was away on a trip.

The committee decided, first of all, that there was no such thing as 'animal magnetism'! Although they admitted that some very interesting and unexplained things happened, in general they denounced the theory and practice. Franklin noted that the effects of animal magnetism were apparently due to the participants' imagination. He did not realize it, but he had hit upon something important if only he had followed it up. He had anticipated the study of psychosomatic medicine by nearly two centuries, but did not appreciate the significance of his own observations! Mesmer was pretty much discredited. The press gave him a very hard time and the public began to lose confidence in him, so he left Paris and lived out the rest of his life in Geneva.

However, Mesmer was a good man who did not enrich himself by his techniques, at least no more so than any other physician. He did not need to, for he did not need the money; he was not only wealthy himself, but also had married a wealthy woman. Mesmer had set up free treatment centres all over the country and there is no evidence that he was motivated by self-aggrandizement, which many stories about him imply.

Abbé Faria

There was another important man at that time, a Portuguese monk named Abbé Faria (1766-1819), who took Mesmerism one step further. He said the phenomenon was caused by concentration, not magnetism. To him, the Mesmerizer or magnetizer was a 'concentrator', and the subject was the 'concentratee', or the one who was concentrated on.

The Abbé Faria was a mysterious figure and people assumed that he had studied in the Orient and mastered yoga, etc. (Although there is no proof that he ever left Europe, he never bothered to correct his imposing public 'image'.) He was a tall, thin, ascetic-looking man with deep-set eyes, a penetrating gaze, a bronze-coloured skin, and a very poised, mystical air about him. He held demonstrations throughout France and other countries. His method basically was to transfix someone with his gaze for a while and at the opportune moment he would shout 'Sleep!' He found that three out of five people would go into exactly the same condition known previously as a 'Mesmeric trance'. The Abbé Faria made a very interesting observation when he said, 'It appears that men can be charmed into illness and charmed into health', which was a very penetrating observation.

Mesmer's idea of 'animal magnetism' has so influenced hypnotism that it is important to understand the basic premise. The premise was that the power lies within the Mesmerizer (the person doing the procedure) and some people are successful at it because they have more of this power ('magnetism') than others. Mesmerism is the idea that some magnetic force emanates from one person to another. This concept has been largely discredited for over two hundred years, but it had a very important influence in terms of metaphysical and psychic theories, and on the thinking of the public even to this day.

The Braid Period

The next stage in the history of hypnosis was the Braid period, from 1842 to 1860. James Braid (1795-1860) was a medical doctor in England who, like many others, had heard of Mesmerism and read a few books on the subject. He was very impressed with some demonstrations by a Mesmerist named LaFontaine.

Braid was an eye-specialist, and one day he said to a patient, 'I want you to look at this very bright light because I want to test your pupillary reflexes.' Just then someone knocked on the door and he remembered that he had a previous appointment which had slipped his mind completely. He told his patient to wait for him and promised to be back as soon as possible.

Braid became so occupied with the second patient that the first patient decided that as the doctor wanted to test his pupillary reflexes, he would save some time by staring at the light while he was waiting. Braid became so engrossed with the second patient that he forgot all about patient number one. As he said good-bye to the second patient, it suddenly dawned on him and he remembered that he had left the poor man sitting in the examining room all the time! He rushed in and saw the man sitting with a glazed look which Braid immediately recognized as a Mesmeric trance! He rushed to a doctor next door and brought him back to show him the man in his office who had gone into a Mesmeric trance by looking at a light.

As they both looked at the man, Braid turned to the other doctor to make a remark and was surprised to see that the doctor was also showing the signs of impending trance! From looking at the patient, he too was staring at the light, and perhaps influenced by Braid's indirect suggestion, was fast becoming entranced!

Braid began to realize that he had discovered a principle which no one else had seemed to grasp. He thought back to LaFontaine's demonstrations and remembered that as people were being magnetized, there was a point at which they got a certain characteristic look in their eyes. The eyelids had fluttered, and the eyeballs rolled up a little as the eyes started to close. Just as a barber notices people's haircuts, or a shoe salesman notices shoes, it was to be expected that Braid, being an eye doctor, would notice people's eyes as they became Mesmerized.

Braid discovered that people could become entranced by looking at a light. He called this phenomenon 'hypnotism' (the word actually originated with James Braid) from the Greek word 'hypno' which meant 'sleep'. He understood that it was a 'lucid sleep' rather than a natural sleep, and he soon realized that 'hypnotism' was a misleading term. He tried to change it, but by that time it had gained such great popularity that we are still stuck with it to this day. Hypnotism has nothing really to do with sleep, but Braid gave us the term and began the whole idea of looking at bright lights and shiny objects to become hypnotized.

Now you can understand how this idea took over, to the extent that in today's television and films nobody is ever hypnotized without a light or some kind of fascination object to stare at. Braid discovered that by eye-fixation on a bright object, within three minutes to three hours people would go into a trance. Of course, he soon realized this was not entirely due to the light. Perhaps as a youngster you read a little book on hypnotism and followed its advice by staring at a light; I certainly did. When I was about fourteen years old, I spent a lot of time staring at bright lights trying to see what would happen. All I can tell you is that staring at bright lights for long periods of time is very, very boring! Apparently that was the main value of it.

Braid soon found he could accelerate this process by telling the person, 'Now you are getting very, very sleepy'. Verbal suggestions speeded it up. The eye-fixation and the bright lights just tired the eyes and overcame a person's resistance.

Dr Elliotson and Dr Esdaile

The Braid period also included men like Elliotson (1791-1868), a medical doctor who popularized the medical uses of hypnotism. Although he was very much persecuted by the medical doctors of his day, Elliotson had a world-wide influence through his publication *The Zoist*, a medical journal devoted to Mesmerism and hypnotism. Another famous man in hypnotism was a physician from Scotland named James Esdaile (1818-1859), who practised medicine in India. He had never actually seen anyone hypnotized, but he had read an article in *The Zoist*. In Calcutta, he began hypnotizing patients for surgery at a time when anaesthesia as we know it today did not exist. He was able to induce deep anaesthesia through hypnosis alone, and performed over three hundred major operations and thousands of minor ones with hypnosis as the only anaesthesia. (At that time, the mortality rate for major surgery was fifty per cent; when people were cut open, they had an even chance of surviving the operation, to say nothing of surviving their illness! Inasmuch as surgeons washed their hands after operations rather than before them, it is a wonder that anyone survived.) By using this technique, James Esdaile reduced the surgical mortality rate in his hospital from fifty per cent to an unheard of five per cent!

When he returned to England, Esdaile read his paper to the British Medical Society; but they laughed him to scorn! They believed that he had been out in the hot sun too long. It probably did not happen, but if it did, it should not have! That would be interfering with nature. Pain is essential. God created pain. It is important for people to feel pain; it builds character, purifies the soul, etc. Esdaile lived out his life a broken man, because few recognized his fantastic accomplishments. Then about that time (the mid-1800s), chemical anaesthesia came into being. (Doctors soon changed their minds about pain alleviation when it involved drugs instead of hypnosis!)

Anaesthesia Discovered

At first, nitrous oxide was not used for anaesthesia; it was just 'laughing gas'. Like degenerated Mesmerism and hypnotism, it was used in sideshows and on stage to entertain the public. People would come on stage, take a whiff of laughing gas, giggle and act silly, and often pass out. The audiences thought it was hilarious. It was years before dentists realized that they could do painless extractions and fillings with it. It was about this time (the mid-1800s) that the anaesthetic properties of chloroform and ether were also discovered.

At the time that Esdaile worked his hypnotic miracles in India, the United States was suffering the ordeal of the Civil War between the States. In those days — as dramatically depicted in the classic movie 'Gone With The Wind' — when doctors amputated a leg, they told the soldiers 'Drink the whisky and bite the bullet, and good luck!' Then they sawed away. Think of the agonies that could have been prevented if their communication technology could have reported Esdaile's successes!

As physicians embraced chemical anaesthetics, the public remained wary until Queen Victoria used it when delivering her baby. Then it became the 'Queen's anaesthetic' and everyone wanted it! Surgeons swung to an extreme. Knowing nothing about the body's tolerance or saturation point for the chemicals, they just soaked a cloth with ether or chloroform, put it over the patient's face and held it there during the operation, pouring on more as they went along. Nurses gave the anaesthetics, as did orderlies, errand boys, or whoever else was at hand. In the early days of anaesthetics, its use was not controlled at all. Surgeons were performing new operating techniques that they had not been able to do before, but patients often died from the anaesthetics! Even in the first decades of the 1900s, this practice continued. It was during that time that an expression we've all heard became popular, 'The operation was a success, but the patient died!'

All this is mentioned only to show that the discovery of anaesthetics served to push Esdaile's work further into oblivion, at a time when it was desperately needed in the world of medicine. This was a major setback for hypnosis.

The Suggestion Period

The period following the Braid period (which emphasized eye-fixation) was the Suggestion period, from 1860 to 1910. Now the emphasis moved away from the idea that there was power in the hypnotist or Mesmerist, and away from the idea that great concentration was needed on the part of the hypnotizer. Even during the time of Braid, Elliotson and Esdaile some hypnotists had begun to realize that it was not so much the fixation of the eyes as a concentration of the subject's attention that was important. A gradual shift was underway in understanding hypnosis.

Charcot

Around 1890 in France, M Charcot began conducting experiments in a psychiatric hospital. He used the noise caused by smashing a gong, and the blinding flashes of photographers' powder, to put his hysterical patients into cataleptic trances. He concluded that only hysterical people could be hypnotized; hypnosis was a symptom of hysteria. However, because those were the only kind of patients with whom he had experimented, he had little chance to test his theory.

Charcot had the idea that there were certain areas of the body called hypnogenic zones which could be touched or stroked to stimulate nerve pathways and induce hypnosis. To him, verbal suggestions were superfluous; by an assault on a person's nervous system, hypnotic trances could be induced.

Charcot also had the strange idea that a hypnotized person was deaf and could not hear suggestions! He gave demonstrations and said, 'Now, doctors, when I stroke this patient's arm it becomes absolutely helpless and paralysed.' When it did, he believed that it was due to the stroking rather than the suggestion. This misconception, that a hypnotized person was 'out of it' altogether, was very common because none of the Mesmerists had ever been Mesmerized; until after World War II, few hypnotists had ever been hypnotized! Therefore, they knew hypnotism from the outside in, rather than from the inside out. This caused the early hypnotists to misunderstand the nature of hypnosis.

Charcot did make contributions to hypnosis, however imperfect according to modern standards. He was the first to classify the depth of hypnosis, saying that there were three levels: catalepsy, lethargy and somnambulism. (This is no longer believed.) He was also the first to apply the word 'somnambulism' to the field of hypnosis, although this was a term which obscured as much as it illuminated as it perpetuated the idea that hypnosis was a kind of sleep.

Bernheim

Two contemporaries of Charcot, Liébeault (1823-1904) and Bernheim (1843-1917), were far more scientific, or at least more modern. They carried hypnosis further than Charcot did. Bernheim understood that there were different susceptibilities to hypnosis among normal subjects and they responded differently from each other.

The Bernheim technique was much more like those used in clinical work today. He originated the soft soothing, lullaby kind of induction. This took induction techniques away from all the noisy hoopla and huff-and-puff showmanship of authoritarian methods. Bernheim popularized the soothing, permissive induction that leads to a relaxed trance which is almost exclusively characteristic of modern clinical practice.

Coué

The most important and least appreciated figure in the Suggestion period was a pharmacist, Emile Coué (1857-1926). He is associated with the phrase, 'Every day in every way, I'm getting better and better'. This practice was called Couéism, and enjoyed a temporary popularity in the United States in the 1920s.

Emile Coué came upon his great discovery when a man came into his pharmacy complaining about his condition. This chronic complainer asked Coué, 'Don't you have any new medicine for this condition? I've tried all your usual powders and tonics. What's wrong with the state of medicine today? Have you anything that can help me?' Coué replied, 'Well, here's something new that just arrived from Paris. They say it's very powerful and I'm sure it will help you. Take it and it will do you good!'

A few days later the man came into the shop hopping and dancing with joy, announcing, 'I'm cured! That's the most wonderful medicine I've ever taken, just look at me!' Coué thought, 'This is a marvellous thing; I'd better analyse it and find out what the 'miracle ingredient' is, for there certainly has to be one!'

He began a chemical analysis in his laboratory and much to his amazement could find nothing in the medicine which by the remotest stretch of the imagination accounted for the results. Yet the man was cured! Coué mentally reviewed his conversation with the man, wondering, 'What happened? What did the man say to me and what did I say to him? What was his state of mind when he took this medicine?' As he analysed his remarks instead of the medicine, he concluded, 'This is a marvellous, miraculous thing — the power of suggestion! Something I said in an off-hand way produced this result!' So Coué began to study the phenomena of susceptibility to suggestion and it led to a major breakthrough in the history of hypnotism.

Bernheim realized, as had Braid, that it was not 'magnetism' from the hypnotist which caused hypnosis, but it was due to the subject's state of mind. The hypnotist had to concentrate the subject's attention, and either this made him more suggestible, or a skilful suggestion made it easier for him to go into a trance. One way or the other, they did not know which, verbal suggestion was the key. Coué made a science out of this.

Autosuggestion

Coué decided this about hypnosis, 'It really isn't the suggestion that the hypnotist gives that accomplishes anything — it's the suggestion that is accepted by the mind of the subject. All effective suggestions must be or become autosuggestions.' To him, hypnosis and self-hypnosis were the same. The man in his shop that day was cured because of what he told himself. He told himself the same thing that Coué told him, to be sure, but it was the man who actually cured himself through his autosuggestion.

Coué began developing this idea and holding free clinics, which will be described later. Coué was not motivated by self-aggrandizement for fame or money, and he did a lot of good. (A man who taught me much of what I know about hypnotism told me that when he was six years old in Germany, Coué visited his home and cured him of bedwetting. He said he could still remember how Coué's great warmth and personal charm made such a profound impression on him.)

However, Coué made one serious mistake — he came to the United States to lecture under the sponsorship of 'hot-shot' promoters who soon oversimplified his teachings to the point of becoming a joke. Comic strip characters like Mickey Mouse, Donald Duck and Popeye were soon saying, 'Every day in every way, I'm getting better and better'. Newspapers held Coué up to public ridicule; perhaps Coué's command of English wasn't sufficient to defend himself to American reporters. At any rate, like many great men before and since, Coué was unjustly dishonoured by the combined ignorance and arrogance of the press. He returned to France to find that the American headlines had arrived ahead of him. He was discredited; people had lost confidence in him, and he could 'do no mightly works'. He became a somewhat broken man by his death in 1926. But he had made a vitally important contribution to hypnotism — he had developed the 'laws of suggestion'.

Post-Pavlovian Period

Beginning around 1904 to the present, hypnotism has been in what we might call a 'post-Pavlovian' or 'neurophysiological' period. Since Pavlov's experiments on conditioned reflexes, there has been a slow but steady emphasis on a neurological interpretation of hypnosis. We are beginning to understand what takes place in the nervous system to create, deepen, manipulate and terminate a hypnotic trance.

The Mesmerists with their 'animal magnetism', Braid with his eye-fixation, Coué with his autosuggestion — all these and the other great men mentioned played a part in the history of hypnotism to the present. Since the 1950s, a tremendous amount of experimental and clinical work has been done all over the world to further our understanding of hypnosis, and much continues to be discovered.

I think this historical perspective will help you to understand better the scope and evolution of hypnotism, so that when you read or hear new things, you will be able to refer to the insights and techniques of the men we have studied and properly evaluate and integrate them into a comprehensive picture. It helps to know something of the historical contexts in which these men lived and did their great work, so we can better appreciate the debt we owe to them.

3.

Trance: A Scientific Explanation

It is usually difficult to discuss the subject of 'trance' because the word has become so commonplace that it has lost any precise definition. In discussions about hypnosis, it is common to hear people talking about trance as if they actually know what they are talking about. However, if you ask, 'What do you mean? What is a trance?', it becomes obvious right away that they have not the faintest idea.

Like many words, 'trance' is used to cover up our ignorance, to give a name to something so vague as to be otherwise nameless to us. Newspapers often carry articles about someone who committed a murder or other crime while 'in a trance'. This apparently means a mental fog or irrational state. Whenever 'trance' is mentioned on television, it is usually without any specific meaning.

The concept of 'trance' is frequently encountered in books and articles dealing with religious experience, psychedelic experience, psychic phenomena, mysticism and of course, hypnotism. Apparently it is a word that people use to describe a condition which they find hard to understand; giving it a name makes them feel more knowledgeable. However, it is only in the field of hypnosis that the word 'trance' has any real scientific meaning. Serious hypnotists have studied hard to understand the condition called 'trance'. Like the word hypnotism itself, trance also has had such a negative connotation to many people that there has been some effort among hypnotists to get rid of it altogether. In the more serious literature on hypnosis over the last twenty years, there seems to be a definite trend away from using the word 'trance'. Instead, either 'hypnotic state' or 'hypnosis' is used. In like manner, the word 'hypnotism' is found less and less in scientific publications, apparently in an attempt to avoid the negative connotations of many words ending in 'ism'. At present, the word 'hypnosis' is widely used to denote the *process* of hypnotizing, the *subject* of hypnotism, and the *state* of hypnosis itself, which was previously called 'trance'. However, I believe that 'trance' is a meaningful concept and a legitimate term *when understood in the way that I am going to explain*.

The Meaning of 'Trance'

The term 'trance' comes from a middle-English and old French word 'transe', which meant great anxiety and fear, and 'transir', to perish, and the Latin 'transire', to die. It is easy to see where the morbid, negative connotations originated. The term itself referred to death itself or to the morbid anxiety and paralysing fear which preceded death. No wonder the 'trance' came to be feared! (Some believe that the Latin term meant 'transition', but this is a modern way of thinking about death. For thousands of years, death came by wounds from accidents or battle, or from uncontrolled disease. Few of our ancestors died peacefully; death was always horribly grim and frequently agonizing. Thus the word 'trance' originally had death-like qualities.)

Contemporary use of the word 'trance' falls into several categories which have become rather well-defined through common usage. When the word is used today, most people think of it in the following contexts:

1. A state resembling sleep, in which consciousness may remain although voluntary movement is lost.
2. A stunned condition; daze, stupor.
3. A condition of great mental abstraction, especially one induced by religious fervour or mysticism; in recent years, a state induced by chemical means, such as psychedelic drugs.
4. A condition in which a spiritualist medium allegedly loses consciousness and passes under the control of some external force, as for the supposed transmission of a communication from the dead.

As we shall see, the first three definitions can be easily related to hypnosis in its various stages. The fourth definition, it seems to me, obviously refers to the same state as the other three, except that it contains unnecessary inferences. It might well be asked, 'Which of these four definitions can, or should be, considered "hypnotic"?'

First, we must distinguish trance from 'coma', which is prolonged unconsciousness brought on by some pathological condition. A trance is neither unconscious nor sleep. If it were either one, we would not need the word 'trance' at all. One of the biggest barriers many people have in experiencing hypnosis is their expectation (and sometimes insistence!) that it be a state of unconsciousness or sleep! They cannot quite seem to grasp the simple idea that if hypnosis equalled sleep or unconsciousness, then there would be no such thing as hypnosis or hypnotists! To the person who says, 'I don't think I was hypnotized — I heard every word you said', I often answer, 'When you wake up each morning, do you feel you've been hypnotized? If not, why not? After all, if you insist that you must be literally asleep or 'blacked out' and unconscious in order to feel hypnotized, then why don't you feel hypnotized on those occasions when you actually have been asleep or unconscious?'

I hope you see my point, because it is crucial to understanding hypnosis. After explaining the above to the person who just cannot seem to believe in the hypnosis which they have just experienced, sometimes the person will still say vaguely, 'Yes, but I certainly don't feel I was in a trance'. They have no idea how to answer if you then ask, 'What does a trance feel like?'

You can see what a poor word 'trance' is to describe the hypnotic state. After all, if you think a trance is a 'death-like state', you will not be particularly eager to experience it. Even after experiencing the true hypnotic trance, you will have a hard time believing it if you expected to 'die' or 'perish', because you certainly did not do that!

Neurological Alteration

A trance is a state of altered awareness brought about by an alteration of the nervous system. It is a state of consciousness rather than unconsciousness. It is an 'off-conscious' state which may be experienced subjectively in different ways. It is a temporary alteration of the nervous system which is felt as altered awareness and perception. It is the result of certain definite causal factors. The technique of causing this neurological alteration is called a 'hypnotic induction' and the condition that results is called a 'hypnotic trance'.

A state of neurological alteration can be produced in many ways. There are diseases which cause metabolic changes that temporarily alter the nervous system to the point where a person experiences changed awareness and perception. There are numerous drugs and chemical agents which (through their presence, absence, or combinations) can produce neurological alterations resulting in altered states of consciousness. Therefore we can distinguish between three basic types of trances which are different only in the way they are caused. The neurological mechanisms by which they are caused are similar and the end results are identical. It should be pointed out that whatever kind of trance situation we are talking about can be produced by another person (hetero-induced) or by the person himself (auto-induced).

The three basic kinds of trances are:

1. Disease Trance
2. Drug Trance
3. Suggested Trance
    a) Verbally induced
    b) Non-verbally induced

(We might make another classification called the 'Environmental Trance' which is caused by repetitive stimuli such as machine noise, windshield wipers — 'highway hypnosis' — ticking clocks, monotony, etc. However, I think of this as a form of non-verbal suggestion.)

By disease trance, we mean those off-conscious states which are the result of some pathological condition such as infection, fever, hormone or chemical imbalance, etc. When an illness (or the body's reaction in fighting illness) alters a person's conscious awareness, then this is a trance state. Many people would be willing to call it a 'trance-like' state, but this is just playing with words; a trance-like state is a trance state, pure and simple. Again, at this point we must distinguish between trance and coma. The disease trance, like a coma, is caused by some pathological factor. However, a coma is a state of unconsciousness and a trance is never an unconscious state. It is only when the disease results in a temporary alteration of conscious awareness and perception that we can call it a 'disease trance'. Truly unconscious states can never be considered as trances.

The drug trance must meet the same test of definition. It must be an off-conscious rather than an unconscious state. This eliminates from consideration those 'knocked-out' or 'blacked-out' states that some people confuse with hypnosis. A drug which produces total unconsciousness does not produce a drug trance, unless it is regulated to stop working just short of unconsciousness. That is why 'narco-hypnosis' is a rather delicate, tricky, and often disappointing business. It is very hard to control the chemical agents in the right balance, according to the individual's weight and resistance to the drug, in order to get and maintain a state of off-consciousness. Drugs which ordinarily produce unconsciousness, even if used restrictively, produce at best a state of semi-consciousness. The trouble is that semi-consciousness is the next thing to being 'dead to the world'. You can see how difficult it is to bring about the desired, controllable, off-conscious state we call a trance. You should know that what doctors call 'hypnotic drugs' produce sleep, for 'hypno' is Greek for sleep. These do not produce what we mean by a hypnotic trance.

More to the point are the drugs commonly designated 'psychedelic' or 'mind-expanding' hallucinogenic substances. The state experienced makes possible a lengthy period of more or less continuous hallucinations of one kind or another. It is definitely a neurological alteration resulting in changed awareness and perception, and therefore qualifies as an example of a drug trance. To me, the drug trance and the disease trance are so similar in risks and unpredictable aspects that it is foolish to submit willingly to either without an overwhelmingly compelling motive.

The suggestion trance (which can be hetero- or auto-induced) produces a safe off-conscious state through scientific procedures. It is a state capable of great versatility, depending on the abilities and goals of those involved. The suggestion trance is called 'hypnotic' by an accident of history (James Braid thought the name would be an improvement over 'Mesmerism') but perhaps the foregoing discussion has helped to put the hypnotic trance in a context of other similar states of mind, which are caused by different factors.

Regarding the relationship between the phenomena obtained by electrical stimulation of the brain (particularly in the hypothalamus and other diencephalic zones) and that produced by hypnosis, Kretchmer stated in 1954, 'The psychological and somatic functions which, according to experiments, may be attained through hypnotism are approximately the same as can be obtained by organic stimulation of the brain, as revealed by Hess' experiments and corresponding clinical observation on man.' Quoted by P. Gloor in 'Autonomic Functions of the Diencephalon. A summary of the experimental work of Professor W. R. Hess,' A.M.A. *Archs. Neurol. Psychiatry,* 71, 773, 1954.)

I hope you can see by now that the nature and phenomena of the trance (produced by whatever means) can be adequately and scientifically explained on a neurological basis. We just do not need to resort to vague supernatural concepts to describe or discuss a natural phenomenon such as the trance.

Two Kinds of Trances

The morbid and negative connotations originally given to the word 'trance' have some basis in fact, according to neurological studies of the trance state. Depending on the kind of stimulation used, two distinct types of hypnotic trances are possible. Anatol Milechnin (in his book *Hypnosis*, 1967) calls these 'trophotropic' and 'ergotropic'. It is simpler to think of them as positive and negative trances.

By negative trances, we mean those caused by stimulating negative emotions, or emotions of a disturbing type, such as fear, etc. Positive trances are the result of stimulating positive emotions, or emotions of the stabilizing type. The positive trance is always beneficial to the nervous system, but the negative trance can be both disturbing and damaging. The positive trance is characterized by relaxation and a sense of peace and tranquillity, whereas the negative trance may be characterized by tension, rigidity and a sense of frustration.

You will remember that the trances described in Mesmer's time were sometimes rather frightening. Mesmeric trances were often characterized by convulsive behaviour, catalepsy, and other rather negative phenomena of the disturbing type. Although Mesmer believed this convulsive element or 'crisis' was an essential part of the treatment, that is like a modern psychiatrist or psychologist who thinks that every patient should go through an abreaction or catharsis.

Even in Freud's time, the demonstrated trances were usually of the negative type. Freud studied hypnosis briefly under Charcot at the Salpêtrière asylum where trances were induced in hysterical patients by exploding a flash of photographers' powder or sounding a loud gong. Most of Charcot's trances could be described as cataleptic today and their distinguishing factor was their negative aspect. No wonder Charcot considered hypnotism to be a pathological symptom of hysteria! Many descriptions of trances in the older literature on hypnosis strike the modern reader as very bizarre. Today, the negative trance is seldom induced deliberately.

You will also remember that Bernheim was the first to change the nature of the trance from negative to positive by using an induction method which stimulated the stabilizing emotions. He accomplished this through a soft, lullaby type of induction which some writers have called 'mother hypnotism', as opposed to the strict, authoritarian type of negative stimulation they call 'father hypnotism' after the stereotypically stern European father.

Stage hypnotists often use authoritarian techniques designed to 'shock' the subject into instantaneous trance. Since this is a stimulation of negative emotions, it results in a negative trance. The negative trance of the stage hypnotist (basically like spontaneous trances caused by traumatic experiences) has become the stereotype or prototype of the hypnotic trance to the average citizen. It is unfortunate that the public is largely ignorant of the positive trance, because it perpetuates a fear of hypnosis.

The Sympathetic and Parasympathetic Nervous Systems

The negative trance is caused by the stimulation of the disturbing emotions; it is really a kind of 'shock' reaction of the sympathetic nervous system. The sympathetic nervous system causes reactions in the body which are related to 'fight or flight'. In other words, it prepares the body to deal with emergencies. These reactions are perceived by us as sensations of excitement and stimulation of fear-related emotions.

The bodily changes that may take place with this kind of stimulation of the sympathetic nervous system are as follows:

1. Acceleration of the heart-rate, with systolic reinforcement.
2. Contraction of the smaller arteries, particularly in the visceral area and in the skin, directing the blood towards the muscles and nervous centres; a possible increase in blood pressure.
3. Dilation of the bronchi, with deeper and quicker breathing, prolongation of the inspiratory phase in comparison with the total respiratory cycle, and increase in pulmonary ventilation.
4. Increase in perspiration, with a corresponding increase in the electrical conductivity of the skin.
5. Pupillary dilation with a tendency towards a larger opening of the eyelids.
6. Decrease in the secretion of saliva.
7. Contraction of the muscular fibres of the skin.
8. Retardation of gastro-intestinal peristaltic movements.
9. Contraction of the bladder.
10. Increase in blood sugar because of a greater destruction of glycogen in the liver.
11. Increase in red cells of the blood due to a contraction of the spleen, with a certain increase in white cells, predominately

myelocytes, and a relative decrease of lymphocytes.
12. Predominance of calcium over potassium and a tendency toward acidosis.
13. Changes in the colloids of the blood.
14. Some increase in adrenalin and thyroid secretions.

It is easy to see that these are reactions which are associated with fear and other negative emotions. This kind of stimulation leads to trances of the negative type. This was the predominant kind of hypnotic trance up until the time of Bernheim.

Animal Hypnosis

The interesting but little-known phenomenon of 'animal hypnosis' falls into the category of the negative trance because it is caused by a stimulation of the negative 'emotions' of the animal. Animal hypnosis has been extensively described by researchers like Schwartz and Bickford in 1956 and by Volgyesi in 1963. (If you are interested in the subject, I can highly recommend *Hypnosis of Men and Animals*, by Volgyesi.)

The 'hypnosis' achieved with animals is best understood as cataleptic immobilization obtained by suddenly placing the animal in an unnatural position. This is the method routinely used in laboratory experiments.

Theoretically, trances of the positive type could be induced in the higher animals (Volgyesi's book has photographs of this) but there are many variables to be controlled. Milechnin and Solovey reported, in 1967, some success in inducing the positive trance in large dogs which were their household pets.

Positive Parasympathetic Trance

The bodily changes which may take place with a stimulation of the parasympathetic nervous system are as follows:

1. Decrease in heart-rate.
2. Vascular dilation, particularly in the visceral area.
3. Increase in the tonus of bronchia muscles.
4. Increase in lacrimal and salivary secretion.
5. Contraction of the pupil.
6. Stimulation of digestive activity.
7. Increase in tonus and movements of the urinary tract.

8. Increase in the quantity of glycogen deposited in the liver and muscles.
9. Tendency towards a decrease in white blood cells, with an increase in eosinophils and lymphocytes.
10. Tendency towards alkalosis.
11. Some increase in insulin, parathyroid, and thymus secretions.

It is easy to see that these are somewhat opposite or complementary reactions to those mentioned with the sympathetic system. The parasympathetic nervous system deals with restorative functions and the storage of resources which may be necessary to deal with difficult situations.

Signs of Hypnosis

The question is often asked, 'How can you tell when a person is hypnotized?' An experienced hypnotist can do this simply by observing the subject. Depending on the characteristics of the type of trance (which is determined by the kind of induction, positive or negative type), a hypnotist learns through experience to associate some changes in the subject's appearance with the onset of hypnosis.

Dave Elman, a great American hypnotist, taught that a hypnotized person gave off 'signs of hypnosis' which could not be faked. These 'signs of hypnosis' could be noticed by a knowledgeable hypnotist at a glance. Elman's 'signs' were such things as bodily warmth, increased lacrimation, a slight reddening of the whites of the eyes upon 'wakening', and eyelid flutter and a tendency for the eyeballs to roll upward. These are physical reactions one would expect from a positive trance induced by stimulation of the parasympathetic nervous system. Bernheim mentioned that a subject's sensation of 'warmth in the pit of the stomach' was a good sign of hypnosis. You can see that this is due to the vascular dilation in the viscera. I have often noticed a subject's compulsive swallowing at an early stage of a hypnotic induction; this is due to the increased salivation caused by stimulation of the parasympathetic nervous system. (There are ways to test the depth of a hypnotic trance, but the trance itself can be recognized by the appearance of certain physical symptoms associated with the stimulation of the parasympathetic system.)

You may be wondering where one might see the kinds of negative trance (produced by stimulation of the sympathetic nervous system) obtained by Mesmer, Charcot, etc. Stage hypnotists often induce this kind of trance, due to their authoritarian induction methods. Trances associated with witchcraft and voodoo practices or primitive rituals are usually of the negative type.

Dr David Akstein, in Brazil, has used the negative trance as a form of abreactive group therapy with selected patients. In Brazil there is an Afro-Brazilian cult, called the Matumba or Macumba sect, whose meetings are characterized by 'possession phenomena' produced amid ritual chanting, drumming and dancing. Dr Akstein has discovered the hypnotic principles underlying this so-called mystical phenomenon (the physiological correlates of sympathetic nervous system stimulation) and has reproduced these kinetic trances for medical purposes. Most clinical hypnotists, however, try to avoid the negative trance with its sympathetic nervous system 'shock', and prefer instead to induce the positive or relaxed trance.

Space does not permit a full exposition of the neurological explanation of trance phenomena, but enough has been explained to show that trances of the negative type are found in frightened animals and in primitive peoples during tribal rituals. The positive trance used in modern clinical practice has also been proved to be a neurological alteration. Therefore, it should be easy to see that there is no need to resort to vague, philosophical, mythological, metaphysical theories or terminology to define and discuss the subject of hypnotic trance. The hypnotic trance must be understood for what it is — a temporary neurological alteration brought about by identifiable natural causes. This understanding clears up the mystery about the trance state observed in both men and animals, which until recently was attributed to unexplained or even supernatural causes.

The Curative Value of Trance

Many writers on hypnosis, especially in the United States, often feel obligated to state that there is no therapeutic value in the trance state *per se*, but these depend on the verbal suggestions given under hypnosis. This belief ought to be challenged until it is modified. Soviet hypnologists, according to Platonov, believe that there is a great benefit in prolonged hypnotic 'sleep'. In the Soviet Union, hypnotherapy sessions are followed by a period of 'suggested sleep' or trance, undisturbed by suggestions. This state continues until the subject spontaneously comes out of it, perhaps in ten minutes or up to two hours. During this time the subject is left absolutely alone.

To American hypnotists who are usually unfamiliar with Pavlovian concepts of hypnosis, this period of suggested sleep is considered to 'set' or 'fix' the therapeutic suggestions more deeply into the subconscious mind. This may be true, but I think there is evidence that the trance state (assuming it to be of the positive type) can have curative properties in and of itself.

The Youth Pill and the Positive Trance

The so-called 'youth pill' known as KH.3 (and other designations) has been widely used in parts of Europe. Developed by Dr Ana Aslan, director of the Geriatric Institute in Bucharest in 1951, the pill dramatically reduced the symptoms of ageing. It caused old people's sense of humour to return, hair to grow in its natural colour, and even favourably affect some (then) untreatable diseases, such as Parkinson's disease.

There are perhaps as many as twenty hormone-based rejuvenators selling in Switzerland, but KH.3 is sold in fifty-five countries and is not a hormone type of pill at all. Surprisingly enough, it is composed of Procaine and Haematoporphyril. The latter is a catalyst which has been used for many years in treating depression; it stimulates the brain and nervous system to make the Procaine work faster. What is this miracle substance, Procaine? It has been known as a pain-killer since 1905. In the United States it is widely used by dentists under the trade name *Xylocaine*! If we have had any dental work done at all, most of us have had it at one time or another.

Although slightly toxic over a long period of time, Procaine rejuvenates the central nervous system. To give you an idea of the possibilities, Dr Aslan reported that one of the 7,000 patients treated with Procaine, a man named Margossjan, entered the hospital at the age of 106. He was bedridden, but after treatment with Procaine he could leave his bed and go for long daily walks. The brown spots on his face disappeared and his white hair became darker. More surprisingly, he regained full command of seven Oriental languages he had spoken before ageing. He finally died at the age of 115!

If you consider all of the physiological changes that occur in the positive hypnotic trance under the stimulation of the parasympathetic nervous system, I think you will agree that we can say the positive trance *is* beneficial 'in and of itself' and may even hold considerable promise as a restorer and rejuvenator of the nervous system — a sort of 'youth pill' without toxic side-effects!

I predict that someday hypnosis (in a disguised form, no doubt) will be a routine treatment in geriatric patients for this very reason.

Trance Depth

The matter of 'depth' of trance should be considered, not from artificial and statistically derived 'scales of hypnotizability' so often published, but from scientifically demonstrable levels of intensified emotional reactions. Therefore, these 'levels' reflect internal alterations in the physiological, biochemical and neurological functions, as well as by mere external changes in the subject's behaviour.

Hypnotic trance can be considered a phenomenon which naturally occurs on a continuum of emotional intensity. I think the terms 'depth' and 'levels' are misleading to the serious student, and I suggest that the more neutral word 'phase' be used.

1. The first phase of intensity of emotional reactions is the normal state of the organism. If the stabilizing emotions are predominant, there is a condition usually described as one of well-being, tranquillity, repose, etc., such as we experience while listening to music, quietly reading, fishing, or any other peaceful and relaxing activity. If disturbing emotions predominate, at this phase they are perceived merely as exhilarating, bracing, exciting, etc.

2. The second phase of intensity of emotional reactions corresponds to the first phase of hypnotic 'depth'. At this point there is some definite change in the person's behaviour and functioning. It may be an increase or decrease in memory, judgement, etc., or an extraordinary mobilization of strength and resistance, and a responsiveness to suggestions of various sorts. It is this phase of intensity usually observed in crowd behaviour or 'mob psychology', and is also the phase of intensity most religious people feel in religious services. This is the state a person experiences at a good film where the combination of muscular relaxation, relative immobility, limitation of the field of vision, and an emotional identification with the actors on the screen produces a state which actually corresponds to the deliberately induced hypnotic state during its earliest stage. The same condition is often reached during psychotherapy and counselling. It is the first phase of hypnosis, sometimes called hypnoidal relaxation or 'waking' hypnosis.

3. The third phase of intensity of emotional reactions corresponds to the second phase of hypnotic 'depth'. At this point there are

gross changes in behaviour, characterized by such things as muscular inhibition, somnambulism, catalepsy and analgesia or anaesthesia.

4. The fourth phase of intensity of emotional reactions is the maximum intensity that has been reached (by either a stabilizing or disturbing emotion), and results in a virtual paralysis of everyday functions. This appears as a 'suspended animation' or a state of extreme lethargy. This corresponds to the third phase of hypnosis which is known variously as 'deep hypnosis', 'catatonic trance', 'plenary state', or the 'Esdaile state'. Neurologically speaking, this phase represents an extreme stimulation of either the sympathetic or parasympathetic nervous system, depending on whether disturbing or stabilizing emotions have been intensified.

In other words, there are four discernible phases of a person's emotional state and there are three phases of hypnosis.

As a person's emotional state is progressively intensified, hypnotic phenomena appear. Depending on the type of emotions which are stimulated, the hypnotic trance which results can be classified as positive or negative. The hypnotic state has three gradations or phases, with the first phase of hypnosis beginning at the second phase of emotional intensity. To summarize:

1. Normal. No hypnosis existing.

2. Slight change from normal behaviour. First phase of hypnosis. Mob or crowd psychology. Imitativeness and suggestibility increases.

3. More change. Second phase of hypnosis. Profound muscular inhibition, analgesia, hallucination, 'somnambulism'.

4. Extreme change. Third phase of hypnosis. Stupor, 'suspended animation', anaesthesia.

Some books on hypnosis teach four levels of hypnosis, which they designate as — light, medium, deep and catatonic. Actually, the phase they designate as 'medium' is best understood as 'artificial somnambulism'. It is a state which looks like true hypnotic somnambulism, but isn't; it appears deeper than it is. If you count it as a true phase of hypnosis, you must add a fourth category to account for the truly deep phase. This four-fold division of trance just does not make sense because it does not correspond to the discernible phases of emotional intensity. You would have to put that so-called 'medium stage' at phase two-and-a-half.

'Deepening' a hypnotic state is therefore best understood as a matter of continued stimulation of the nervous system. The qualities of the trance will depend on the innate and acquired abilities of the subject, on the environment, and on the kind of stimulation used.

Categorizing the Hypnotic Subject

Bernheim was the first to point out that subjects differed in their susceptibility to hypnosis. Hypnotists who work with only one kind of subject (the 'easy' one) never bother to study this topic. Not understanding the true nature of the differences between people, they dismiss many would-be subjects by calling them resistant, refractory, unable to concentrate, etc.

Just as the trance is understood scientifically in terms of the changes that temporarily occur in the nervous system, so the person being hypnotized must be understood in terms of the type of nervous temperament he brings to the induction experience. In short, we should understand not only the type of stimulation used, but also the nervous system being stimulated.

Hippocrates, the 'Father of Medicine', classified people into four types according to their temperaments. ('Temperament' is another way of saying 'nervous system type'.) However, Hippocrates did not know much about the nervous system. He thought there were fluids, which he called 'humours', that predominated in a body. Whichever 'humour' or fluid predominated determined the emotional characteristics of that person. His four-fold classification was as follows:

1. Choleric
2. Sanguine
3. Melancholic
4. Phlegmatic

Pavlov and his Dogs

The Russian physiologist, Ivan Pavlov, conducted his famous experiments on conditioned reflexes with dogs. He soon found that some dogs could be conditioned (or deconditioned) much faster than others. Some dogs could be made 'neurotic' or 'psychotic' easier and faster than others. Of these dogs, certain ones could be cured or rehabilitated faster than others. This meant that not all experimental animals responded equally to the same stimuli. Neither all dogs nor all humans respond to the same stimuli in an identical manner. Although the mechanisms of the conditioned reflex were the same, there were modifications of response due to the differing types of nervous systems.

Pavlov explained practically everything in terms of 'excitation' or 'inhibition' of the nervous system. For example, when you see the light is green and you step off the curb to cross the street, it is an example of an 'excitatory' reflex or response. But if you see a car approaching rapidly, you immediately step back on the curb, due to an 'inhibitory' reflex.

As he worked with his dogs to establish conditioned reflexes of various sorts (he is most famous for conditioning dogs to salivate at the sound of a bell) and noticed the difference in the ease with which various dogs were conditioned, he soon divided his dogs into two major groups. It seemed that all dogs were either 'excitatory' or 'inhibitory' in their nervous temperaments. It would take five to eight times more sedatives to calm a dog of a strong 'excitatory' type than it would to calm a dog of the weak 'inhibitory' type with the same body weight.

However, he soon discovered through experimentation that there were two sub-divisions within those two major categories, making a four-fold classification of nervous temperaments. Since these were descriptive of nervous temperaments, they applied equally to humans. Pavlov's classification was as follows:

1. Excitatory —
   a) Strong excitatory
   b) Lively excitatory
2. Inhibitory —
   a) Calm, imperturbable
   b) Weak inhibitory

When dogs of all types were subjected to more stress (intensified stimulation of the disturbing type) than they could cope with, they eventually ended up with states of 'brain inhibition' (negative trance), which Pavlov considered to be a protective mechanism of nature, designed to protect the brain as a last resort when pressed beyond endurance. However, the point is that dogs of the 'weak inhibitory' type went into this state very quickly and in response to much lighter stresses. This finding later had great significance in what came to be known as 'brainwashing'.

Inasmuch as the hypnotic trance is a state of neurological alteration, brought about by the stimulation of emotions of either the disturbing or stabilizing type, then it follows that the susceptibility of a person to hypnosis would naturally depend on his 'nervous system' or neurological type.

A Hypnotist and His Subjects

Stage hypnotists soon learned that not everyone was equally susceptible to their techniques, nor equally capable of the kind of hypnotic phenomena necessary for a 'good show' in public. Driven by the necessity of weeding out those who responded slowly, if at all, to standard induction techniques, the stage performer used 'suggestibility tests' to select quickly the most responsive subjects. The very fact that the people volunteered was part of the selection process. By rapid testing, the hypnotist soon had several subjects he could rely on to behave in a predictable manner. Therefore, the stage hypnotist really considered people to be in one of two categories: the 'good' subjects and the 'bad' ones.

A doctor who took up the study of hypnosis had to take his lessons from the lay hypnotist or stage performer in the beginning and it was natural that he learned the same selection techniques which presupposed that people were either good or bad subjects for hypnosis. The doctor felt that he could not waste too much time either. So in the process of utilizing hypnosis in a small selected number of patients, he necessarily eliminated many as 'bad' subjects, and thereby unwittingly deprived them of the benefits of hypnosis.

The clinical hypnotist who specialized to a greater extent in hypnotherapy had to work with nearly everyone who came to him; he could not pick and choose his subjects like the fast-paced entertainer or the busy doctor. His temperament was disposed to spend more time with each individual and to try to teach them to become good hypnotic subjects over a period of time. Out of this new attitude among hypnotists, new techniques of induction and classification of subjects slowly emerged.

Most of these categorizing attempts followed the work of experimental hypnotists in university settings, and ended up with a statistical description of the percentages of students who responded to various graded 'susceptibility tests'. This work could be described as phenomenological rather than neurologically oriented. The difference between hypnotic subjects was considered to be more or less 'just the way it is', without any attempt to correlate it with the various nervous system types.

Sometimes hypnotists would, by observation and experience, reach conclusions about the difference in hypnotizability between male and female subjects, young and old subjects, or differences in occupations, educational or intelligence levels, nationalities, etc. Although operationally valid, these classifications merely attributed differences among hypnotic subjects as due to environmental and developmental differences. In other words, subjects responded differently because of their differing past experiences, attitudes, expectations, etc.

Still, no one seemed able to correlate the findings of Pavlov to the classification of hypnotic subjects. American hypnologists have never been too interested in the physiological approach to hypnosis, but the Pavlovian influence was very strong outside the English-speaking world. European and South American hypnologists are Pavlovian (or neo-Pavlovian, as some prefer, due to recognition of the involvement of subcortical brain structures in hypnosis) and it is from these directions that recent advances along this line have come.

The late Hungarian hypnologist, Dr Ferec Andreas Volgyesi, proposed a typology in this regard. He maintained that there are four basic types of nervous temperament as follows:
1. Constitutionally and developmentally psycho-active.
2. Constitutionally psycho-active but developmentally psycho-passive.
3. Constitutionally psycho-passive, but developmentally psycho-active.
4. Constitutionally and developmentally psycho-passive.

Those in the first category are people who have inherited psycho-active nervous constitutions, and also have acquired psycho-active dispositions through their upbringing. The second category are those people who have inherited a psycho-active constitution, but have acquired psycho-passive dispositions. The third group is composed of those who have inherited psycho-passive constitutions, but have later acquired psycho-active dispositions. People who are psycho-passive both by inherited nervous constitutions and acquired characteristics are in the fourth category. This system should satisfy both sides of the old 'heredity versus environment' debate!

Dr Volgyesi believed that about fifty per cent of educated people fall into Group Four, about twenty-five per cent into Group Three, and twenty per cent into Group Two, with the remaining five per cent in Group One.

Correlating the Types

As we attempt a correlation of the 'types' of people, we should be struck with the fact that there seems to be not only four categories, but that these designations of human temperament seem to be quite compatible with each other. If we synthesize the typologies of Hippocrates, Pavlov and Volgyesi, this is the result:

1. Excitatory (Psycho-active)
    a) Strong excitatory. Inherited psycho-active nervous constitution with further acquired psycho-active disposition. The 'choleric' person.
    b) Lively excitatory. Inherited psycho-active nervous constitution with acquired psycho-passive disposition. The 'sanguine' person.
2. Inhibitory (Psycho-passive)
    a) Calm, imperturbable. Inherited psycho-passive nervous constitution with acquired psycho-active disposition. The 'melancholy' person.
    b) Weak inhibitory. Inherited psycho-passive nervous constitution with further acquired psycho-passive disposition. The 'phlegmatic' person.

This classification deserves serious consideration. It may not coincide with our wishful thinking about the human race, but it is very likely the most scientific classification to date. The Volgyesi percentages are merely approximations, of course, but it is most interesting because hypnotists have always been in agreement that twenty per cent of any population can be easily and deeply hypnotized at the first attempt.

Brain Inhibition and Breakdown

Pavlov found that under gradually increasing stimulation of the stressful or disturbing type, 'abnormal' behaviour would sooner or later appear. This 'abnormal' behaviour (which of course is normal under the abnormal stress) could be divided into three stages as follows:

1. 'Equivalent' stage in which the brain gives the same response to both strong and weak stimuli.
2. 'Paradoxical' stage in which the brain responds more actively

to weak stimuli than to strong stimuli.
3. 'Ultraparadoxical' stage in which conditioned reflexes and behaviour patterns turn from positive to negative, or from negative to positive.

Finally, of course, a stage of 'breakdown' is reached when the limits of the brain's ability to cope at all have been surpassed. It resembles hysterical coma; Pavlov called it 'transmarginal protective inhibition'.

Nervous Dogs and Nervous Men

Certain scientific propositions have resulted from these studies. They apply to all human states of altered awareness whether achieved by exhaustion, traumatic and nerve-wracking emotional experiences, drugs, lack of sleep, negative hypnotic induction or a planned combination of all these factors which has come to be known in our day as 'brainwashing'.
All the experimental data lead to the following propositions:

1. People, like Pavlov's dogs, respond to imposed stresses, increased stimulation, or conflict situations in predictable ways according to their different types of inherited and acquired temperament.

For example, the 'strong excitatory' dog, or the 'choleric' man, or the 'psycho-active/psycho-active' hypnotic subject would respond to extreme stimulation with panic and wild aggression.
The 'lively excitatory' dog, the 'sanguine' man, or the 'psycho-active/psycho-passive' hypnotic subject would respond to the same extreme stress with purposeful, controlled aggression.
The 'calm, imperturbable' dog, the 'melancholy' man, or the 'psycho-passive/psycho-active' hypnotic subject would respond to such stress with passive behaviour.
The 'weak inhibitory' dog, the 'phlegmatic' man, or the 'psycho-passive/psycho-passive' hypnotic subject would respond to the identical stress with avoidance reactions and extremely passive behaviour.
Finally, humans as well as animals break down when stresses or conflicts become too great for their nervous systems to master.

2. Environmental influences produce reactions to normal stress

only in altering certain details of behaviour. The basic temperamental pattern is not changed; 'abnormal' stress forces everyone into predictable reactions.

Pavlov noted that the 'weak inhibitory' dog would experience 'transmarginal protective inhibition' (a 'nervous breakdown' if it happened to a human) much faster than dogs of another type, even with much lighter stresses.

I have mentioned that dogs of the 'strong excitatory' type require doses of sedatives five to eight times greater than those required by a 'weak inhibitory' dog of the same weight. It is common knowledge that drug effects on humans vary widely, in the same way as reactions to normal and abnormal amounts of stress do. Whatever modifications may take place in the behaviour due to different environmental factors, the basic nervous type of the individual is not, and cannot be, changed.

3.   The amount of stress that can be tolerated by a human or a dog of any nervous type depends also on the physical condition of the person or animal.

A lowering of resistance can therefore be produced by such means as fatigue, starvation, fevers, drugs, etc. In the field of hypnotism, the brilliant Abbé Faria made a penetrating observation when he noted that people who had been recently 'bled' (a common medical practice in his day) were more susceptible than usual to Mesmeric induction.

People have been observing other people since the beginning, but it is a quirk of human nature that we carefully observe only that which is unusual and we tend to overlook the commonplace. We study more about disease than we do about health, and more about the abnormalities than we do about the normal conditions. Therefore, much of our observations of the effects of neurological alteration (trance) on behaviour, has been under the abnormal conditions of war, starvation, disease, drugs, and all sorts of unpleasant influences. Yet these studies have led to important knowledge and we should be grateful for it.

Although much of what I have said about the scientific explanation of trance and its related phenomena has been applicable primarily to negative trances, which are produced by stimulating disturbing emotions, these principles can relate to all cases of neurological alteration, including positive hypnotic trance. Serious students of hypnosis will have to apply the implications of these principles to the hypnotic trance of the positive type, which is elicited by stimulating the stabilizing emotions.

Hypnosis is a Science

I hope that this discussion of 'trance' has shed some light on the subject. At least I hope I have established the point that we can best talk about hypnosis in a scientific terminology. It is a mistake to adopt metaphysical terms to describe phenomena which can be defined and described adequately in the accepted language of natural science. To continue speaking about hypnosis in outmoded figures of speech will retard its future scientific development and modern acceptance.

I would urge all hypnologists to learn to think in, and speak, the language of science!

4.
Dangers and Limitations of Hypnotism

I believe we have arrived at the point in this study where we ought to discuss very candidly and very openly the dangers and limitations of hypnotism.

If you ask most hypnotists, 'Is there any danger to hypnotism?' they will answer, 'Oh, no, not at all.' That is not being completely honest. There are potential dangers, and we need to study, analyse and consider them. What do we mean when we talk about dangers? The first main point I would like to make is this: there is *nothing* more dangerous than ignorance!

Danger to the Subject

In every activity of human life there is an element of danger. It is a dangerous thing just to get born into this world because a lot of people get severely damaged in being born. It is a very dangerous thing just to grow up and many people do not make it. It is dangerous to ride a bicycle or to roller-skate, for you might break an arm or leg. It is dangerous to drive a car because there are a lot of accidents. It is dangerous to do just about anything!

Harmful and injurious aspects of life which are scientifically recognized and rationally approached are one thing, but imaginary dangers of witches and vampires are something else. So, let's be sure when we are talking about dangers, that we are not talking about imaginary dangers.

We want to deal with the dangers, or the potentially negative aspects of hypnosis, in terms of dangers to the person who is being hypnotized, and then dangers to the hypnotist. I think the biggest danger in hypnotism is to the hypnotist, not to the subject!

The Illusion of Power

The illusion that hypnosis is a 'power relationship between two people' runs very deep in the public mind. It has been fostered by stage hypnotists because their success depends on the audience believing this. Thus, through the entertainment media, people have this 'Svengali syndrome' in their minds; they really think that hypnotism is a situation where one person is under the 'control' of another. Yet when hypnosis is subjected to rational study, as we are doing, it emerges as anything but a power relationship. The only 'magic' in hypnosis lies in the mind of the subject, not in the mind of the hypnotist. The power of hypnosis (which is considerable) exists only in the mind of the subject!

This should not be too hard to understand. If you ask me if I believe in voodoo and witch doctors and the business of sticking pins in little dolls, making curses and hexes, etc., I can't answer with an unqualified 'yes' or 'no'. I have to qualify my answer. Yes, I believe it works because people do get cursed and sometimes get sick and die. (Whole cultures are based upon this kind of foolishness.) However, no, I do not believe that there is any power in voodoo that is *external to the mind* of the person who believes in it. I just cannot imagine any civilized person believing that. I do not believe a witch doctor has power in himself to do that. I do not believe that there is such power in a combination of ingredients in a love potion. I do not believe that there is power in magic words, etc. I cannot believe that there is literally power in any of this.

Power in the Mind

The power that it has *exists in the mind* of the recipient. Now, there is great power in hypnosis (no one knows it better than me) but it is *in the mind of the subject that is being hypnotized.* All the tremendous things that can be done with hypnosis are done with the power which is inherent in the mechanisms of the mind — that is where the power resides. Since the time of Coué, most honest hypnotists have readily admitted that all hypnosis is really self-hypnosis; that is, it is not the suggestions that are given that necessarily do anything, it is the suggestions that are accepted which do everything. It is not what goes on in the mind of the hypnotist that is important, but what goes on in the mind of the subject! However, stage hypnotists and their kind have a vested interest in strengthening the illusion that hypnosis is a power relationship rather than a co-operative one. This has fostered the fear that hypnosis represents a great danger to the subject — some kind of dehumanizing threat to his humanity, or even a danger to his life or sanity. These are fears based on legends, films or novels and they are just not true.

Hypnosis is achieved by the subject in co-operation with the guidance of the hypnotist; this point cannot be emphasized too much. The person who experiences the hypnotic state is the 'subject' and not the 'object' of hypnosis.

Documented Dangers

You are familiar with the nonsense which appears in the press now and then when somebody claims something sensational about hypnotism and its alleged dangers, such as a person getting hypnotized and nobody can bring him out of it, etc. What truths there are about the dangers of hypnosis will be found in scientific journals and not in the popular press stories about its alleged dangers. In Hilgard's *Hypnotic Susceptibility* (an authentic book based on work done at the Laboratory of Hypnotic Research at Stanford University) there is a chart of 'reported adverse effects of symptom removal through hypnosis'. It lists fourteen cases (and these seem to be the only documented cases in medical history up through 1961) where there were harmful effects of treatment through hypnosis, and this happened only when hypnosis was used as a means of directly removing a symptom without finding and correcting the cause of it.

That book lists the gender and ages of the fourteen subjects, the original symptom treated, and then the severe symptom that later developed (mostly psychotic reactions). Over half of these cases were reported by a Dr Rosen, who was an outspoken critic of hypnotism in the American Medical Association. He was responsible for the minority report of a minority committee to the effect that hypnotism should not only be limited to practice by medical doctors, but even then only to specially-trained psychiatrists. (In his opinion, not even qualified anaesthesiologists, paediatricians, dermatologists, etc., had any business using hypnosis!) It should be pointed out that he stands alone in his contention. His view has never had the support of the medical hypnotists in the whole country. Since he is the man who documented nine of the fourteen cases, it makes us wonder why he (out of thousands of medical hypnotists) saw these types of cases? These cases need to be examined very carefully to see, first of all, whether the later problems which developed had anything to do with the hypnotic treatment. That is debatable.

The same book reports follow-up interviews with students who were used in hypnotic experiments. The interviews were held a few days after the hypnotic inductions. (Remember, these were students in experiments, not patients in therapy.) They made statements like this: 'I was in a fog for one hour,' or, 'Things were hazy and vague for several hours,' etc. One subject, 'continued to be drowsy and felt ill after the first induction and returned the next day in a state of acute anxiety over continuing the experiment.'

The apparent cause of this was the technique used by the experimenters (or perhaps I should say the lack of technique). When people complain of headaches or some other symptom of 'hypnotic hangover', it is due to the lack of knowledge and the improper techniques by the hypnotist. (In university experiments, usually graduate students act as the hypnotists.) Those familiar with stage hypnotism are aware of the fact that many people will later complain of headaches, muscle tension, etc., because in the hypnotic state they were abused in some way, having been asked to do things which were somewhat beyond their physical abilities. It stands to reason that if you are going to induce catalepsy and stretch someone between two chairs and then expect them to support a great weight, you should pick a subject in good physical condition. It just does not make sense to do this to a frail, elderly person. Yet, there are people who think there is such magic in hypnosis that they could fire a bullet through the head of a hypnotized subject and tell him it was not going to hurt! That is naive and stupid. I have made the statement many times that, 'Hypnosis is not dangerous, but some hypnotists are.' Every year I learn that there are some very, very incompetent people practising hypnotism. I refer mainly to those who use it at parties for entertainment, etc.

Another book I want to quote is *Hypnotherapy: Survey of the Literature* by Brenman and Gil. These recognized authorities had this to say:

> Schultz, who made the most systematic investigation of reports of 'injuries due to hypnosis' found that most of these occurred where hypnosis had been used for entertainment, or to satisfy the curiosity of an amateur. Even these injuries were shown to be amenable to appropriate treatment.

They quoted Moll as saying that he had never seen anyone become disturbed as a result of being hypnotized unless exciting suggestions were given irresponsibly, without taking care to restore the person to the normal state gradually. Moll said that the possible danger of bringing about a too-easy susceptibility to hypnosis may be prevented by telling the patient in hypnosis that no one will ever be able to hypnotize him against his will or desire, that he will never experience hypnotic phenomena in the normal state, etc. Bernheim gives substantially the same discussion.

Pierre Janet went so far as to say that he regarded it as unfortunate that there was so little danger attached to hypnosis! He said:

> I say 'unfortunate' for the reason that a medicine is not really potent unless it is able to be dangerous on occasions; and it is very difficult to think of any method of treatment which could be efficacious although it could never by any possibility do harm. The dangers attaching to the use of a poisonous drug make it necessary that we should study with great care how to administer it, and in what doses; but the fact that the drug is poisonous is the primary indication that it is powerful. We can hardly say as much of suggestion and of experimental hypnosis, for, even in bad hands, suggestion and hypnotism do not seem to have been able to do much harm.

Triggering Psychosis

Although there is general agreement that care should be taken to separate clearly the hypnotic and normal states, so that the subject does not carry over into his daily life the reactions that occur in hypnosis, I trust you are beginning to see the panorama of the differences of opinion which have been presented. There are two major dangers which have been discussed in the literature: (1) the possibility that the subject may develop an undue subordination to the hypnotist; and (2) the danger of triggering an incipient psychosis into manifestation. In other words, it is possible to trigger a psychosis in a person who is already a borderline psychotic, a person who is walking a tight-rope between normality and insanity.

However, this is no more a pitfall in hypnotherapy than with other forms of psychotherapy, especially psychoanalysis. As the man said, 'Anybody who goes to a psychiatrist ought to have his head examined.' Some people go and get worse because in dealing with a borderline psychotic you could trigger a psychotic episode not only through hypnosis, but even through an innocent remark in conversation. Such a person could be watching TV, or reading something, and be triggered off. So it really is not fair to single out hypnosis, except that these people should be screened out and not be hypnotized in the first place. Basically, any dangers that do apply, do when direct rather than permissive methods of hypnosis are used.

Hypnosis is Safe

There is one book which I consider to be the greatest single volume on hypnosis in existence. I have learned more from it than any other ten books; I think it is the greatest thing written in two hundred years on the subject of hypnotism. It is *Hypnosis* by Dr Anatol Milechnin. Dr Milechnin practised medicine in Uruguay. I met his wife, Galena Solovey, who is also a world-famous medical hypnotist, at the Panamerican Medical Convention in Buenos Aires in 1967.

Milechnin quotes many famous hypnotists who emphatically assert the complete absence of dangers in therapeutic hypnosis. He quotes Wetterstand (1897) who applied group hypnosis on an enormous scale, filling various rooms in his house with hypnotized patients. Wetterstand declared that he induced the hypnotic state 60,000 times without any unfavourable consequences. Liébeault (1886) summarized his thirty years of medical practice on 10,000 patients by saying that in some of these he had induced the hypnotic state more than 100 times with no harmful effects. Bernheim (1891) had a similar experience with several thousand patients and concluded that therapeutic hypnosis 'often cures, and when it does not cure it improves, and if it is not beneficial it is still completely harmless'. You just cannot be any more emphatic than that!

The people who are most qualified to speak on the dangers of hypnosis are those who have practised hypnosis the most! I can only add that I have conducted more than 20,000 hypnotherapy sessions and I have never seen any of the so-called dangers of hypnotism in my practice.

The Dangers of Authoritarian Hypnosis

However, when we are talking about stage hypnotism or authoritarian methods which stimulate negative emotions, then there are some real dangers. I would like to refer to a case where death was caused under hypnosis by this kind of technique.

According to Volgyesi (1956) a nineteen-year-old Hungarian girl named Ella Salamon died under hypnosis in 1894. She had been successfully treated for nervous disorders by two doctors and an amateur hypnotist named Franz Neukomn. Neukomn felt that the girl had 'mediumistic faculties' and wanted to experiment with her to demonstrate telepathy and clairvoyance.

Before a large audience in Hungary on September 14, 1894, Neukomn gave the girl the following suggestion, the idea being to send her soul to a faraway village to obtain information about a certain sick person: 'I am now sending your soul away from here!' The subject reacted to this order with agitated deep breathing and with inarticulate sounds. It was evident that the order had caused the young woman to experience a strong disturbing emotion. Neukomn continued to insist categorically with this order and the girl died under hypnosis! Neukomn made two mistakes: he gave a command (hardly a suggestion) to which the subject reacted with great fear; and then, instead of finding out what was wrong, he insisted that *he* be obeyed without regard for his subject's discomfort. This is an example of what may happen when the hypnotist is ego-centred instead of client-centred.

The hypnotist Franz Neukomn was accused of homicide and the autopsy reported 'death by heart paralysis'. Fortunately for Neukomn, he was absolved by the court on October 26, 1895 because he had acted with good intentions and had previously achieved therapeutic results with the girl.

Milechnin remarks that some contemporary authors on hypnotism do not take into consideration the possible pathogenic and even fatal consequences of the deliberate stimulation of intense, disturbing emotions in certain subjects, and who then even go so far as to recommend a therapeutic intensification of emotions. Oddly enough, it is psychiatrist Dr Rosen (who finds hypnosis dangerous in the hands of non-psychiatrists) who uses this dangerous procedure. He tells patients under hypnosis that, 'whatever your underlying emotion is at present, you'll gradually feel it grow stronger and stronger still, stronger than you've ever felt it before in all your life, until it's as strong as you're able to bear, until you feel it as deeply as it is possible for you to feel any emotion.' Out of eleven cases with this procedure, he reports a patient who reacted with gestures that indicated a scene of being raped, another subject reacted with trembling, breath-holding, abundant perspiration, etc. Now, this kind of technique may be used in special cases, but there is a risk which must be taken into account by the prudent hypnotist.

The Truth About Dangers

Milechnin goes on to state that the dangers in hypnotic suggestion are the dangers of any interpersonal relationship: if you do not want your mind to be affected, then you should never listen or talk to anybody, because the same dangers you fear in a hypnotic relationship are inherent in every interpersonal relationship you have. Furthermore, any danger from the trance itself is the same danger you have under the stimulation of any strong emotion. It is obvious that hypnosis has been blamed for a lot of things it has nothing to do with.

If a famous film star dies, either as a suicide or 'accidental' death, and it is revealed that she has been under a psychiatrist's care for several years, nobody says, 'Well, that just goes to show what happens when you go to a psychiatrist. If you fool around with those people, you'll go crazy and die of a drug overdose'. People realize how insensitive that would be, so they say, 'Well, this was a sick person and it was a terrible tragedy'. Yet, if the star had had one session of hypnotherapy at any time in the previous five years, it is possible that someone will say, 'Aha! That proves what a dangerous thing it is to fool around with hypnosis!' No one advocates 'fooling around' with hypnosis. These ridiculous charges may sell a lot of tabloid newspapers, but you have to analyse these things and put them into proper perspective.

The Dependence on the Hypnotist

The objection that people may become unduly dependent on a hypnotist is based again on the fallacy that hypnosis is a power relationship. Although this is unlikely in clinical hypnosis, it appears to be a danger in the context of amateur or stage hypnotism because long-continued or frequently repeated inductions seem to result in a certain mental vagueness with some 'somnambulistic' subjects. (Remember, this is the only kind of subject the stage hypnotist deals with.) A somnambulist who works regularly with a stage hypnotist (like a stooge) may indeed be hypnotized in every performance, but he or she is there because the stage performer needs and can count on 'his' somnambulist. He trains and develops them for that purpose. If you ever get acquainted with any of these people, you will notice what I mean by a 'mental vagueness', a certain 'out-of-focus' personality they all have. A somnambulist by nature is highly suggestible and is capable of extreme introversion and induced psychic withdrawal.

Many of these people exhibit this same kind of vagueness in their daily lives *apart from hypnosis* and they have a certain 'detachment from reality' similar to folks with psychic pretensions. (Most psychics have this characteristic in their daily lives.) This mental vagueness is also observed in subjects *whose non-hypnotic relationship with the hypnotist can accurately be described as neurotically dependent and submissive.* In other words, where the hypnotist and the subject are man and wife, or lovers, or something like that in their day-to-day relationship — and the subject is a passive-submissive personality to an extreme degree — this mental vagueness and undue dependency can often be noticed.

None of this should be used as an indictment against hypnosis. The point is, all these dangers to the subject are recognizable and they are all preventable. The average person has nothing to fear from somnambulistic pathology, simply because he is not capable of it; his personality makes it impossible for him to achieve those trance levels except under rare circumstances, such as with skilled guidance and strong motivation for therapeutic purposes. Naturally it should be added that the somnambulist has nothing to fear from the trained and ethical hypnotist who knows his limitations and routinely observes the normal cautions observed by anyone who deals with people on an interpersonal basis.

There is a great advantage to hypnosis: it has the ability to correct its own errors! Problems which may be created by it can also be cured by it; what one ignorant hypnotist might do to damage somebody, a trained hypnotist can correct.

Now I would like to discuss the danger that few people would even imagine existed.

Dangers to the Hypnotist

It would never occur to people who are superstitious or ignorant about hypnosis that there is any danger to the hypnotist himself. This is a real danger because a person who takes up the study and practice of hypnotism can only develop confidence in his ability as a result of successful inductions and, of necessity, the early successes are with the 'good' or 'easy' or 'quick' subjects. If you are a hypnotist who is just beginning, you are going to look for the easiest subjects you can find. When you find one, you are going to be so thrilled that you will never want to let them go. This discovery of your personal 'power' over a hypnotized subject increases your confidence for further success, but herein lies a great danger to you. There is a tendency to spend too much time working with that kind of subject because there is a tendency in all of us to want to repeat ego-satisfying experiences (if it makes us feel good, we want to do it again), so there is a temptation for the novice hypnotist to spend a disproportionate amount of time with easy subjects.

It takes a lot of maturity and mental balance for a hypnotist to keep from getting carried away by this illusion of power. Sometimes it is hard to know who is really getting hypnotized, the subject or the hypnotist! When the hypnotist begins to think *he* really has the power the subject attributes to him, then he is in bad trouble, and that is what I am referring to.

Unconscious Motivations

In the context of possible dangers to the hypnotist, I think it is worthwhile to consider the motives which impel a person to take up the study and practice of hypnotism. As in every other field of study, the motivation can be either that which appeals to the best in people, or to the worst.

Advertisers who spend millions of dollars to sell their clients' products carefully study their markets. Few products are for a general market; most are aimed for a segment of the general market. There is a psychological profile of the buyers of any product or service, and effort is made to design advertising to appeal to their unconscious as well as conscious motivations.

If we analyse the most prevalent kind of advertising used to sell books or tapes on hypnotism, we get a clue to the unconscious motivations of this targeted select market that the advertising is aimed at. If we examine popular adverts for hypnotism, we can answer the question, 'What is the motivation (perhaps unconscious) that impels people to study hypnotism?' The conclusions are not very complimentary.

Sex

Of course, those who write advertising copy are very adept at promising much for so little, and they really outdo themselves when it comes to adverts on hypnotism. They write adverts which are evidently designed to appeal to the inadequate, introverted, immature person who seeks either sex, status, or sociability through the 'magic power' of hypnosis! I think you know the kind of thing I am talking about. Again, this advertising is based on the illusion that hypnosis is a 'power relationship' between two people — which it is not — and cultivates the idea that it is between a male and a female. You have never seen a picture in an advert of a man hypnotizing a man, have you? I haven't, and I don't think we ever will.

The subject is always a very attractive young female model with a low-cut, plunging neckline and soulful eyes, gazing up passively and helplessly at the male hypnotist. It does not take too much imagination to see what the appeal to the public is in this kind of advertising. The appeal is, of course, the implication that hypnosis is a tool for sexual exploitation; it gives you some sort of irresistable personal magnetism which will transform a normally conventional woman into an uninhibited and compliant sexual partner.

Psychic Domination

Other kinds of advertising appeal to the desire to dominate the thoughts of others or to exert a sort of undetected mental control over others' thoughts and actions. This is an appeal to 'psychic dominance'.

This appeal, too, strikes a responsive chord in either very immature people, or rather sick people. No well-adjusted person really seeks to exercise psychic dominance or undetected control over anybody's mind or life. I remember when I was a lad (with the excuse of immaturity) I thought that would be a great thing. I recall talking to my doctor friend who was my first teacher of hypnotism and I mentioned that I wished I could read other people's minds and know their thoughts. Wouldn't that be great? He just shook his head and said, 'No, but you would certainly have a dirty, confused mind!' That deflated me. When you stop to think of the rubbish and trivialities that you would have in your mind if it were filled with what occupies the minds of most people you come into contact with, you would see that it would be a pretty worthless 'gift' to have. It could be more of a burden than a blessing.

Laziness

The advertising that is used to promote self-hypnosis often has an unwholesome emphasis on achieving the unattainable with a minimum effort. The things which are usually the result of good breeding, intensive education, and tireless discipline are all offered by mere relaxation or sleep, practising some kind of postures, or enrolling in a mystical brotherhood, etc. Now, anyone who really expects these things to come that easily is obviously a little bit out of touch with reality.

I am not knocking yoga or esoteric brotherhoods; if that is your interest you are welcome to it. Everything, including hypnosis and self-hypnosis, has reasonable benefits to all serious students; but no intelligent adult really can expect the sun and the moon and the stars for the mere expenditure of the price of a book or booklet, or enrolling in a course.

This does not mean that the people who take up hypnotism are consciously or unconsciously motivated by feelings of inferiority or sexual inadequacy, but this is often the advertising appeal. This must be why there are (let's face it) so many weird people interested in hypnosis. With that kind of advertising, what else could you expect? It is not a scientific, intellectual, or adult appeal. The point is, even in people who have an aptitude for hypnosis, there is a need to be on guard against this childish fascination for the 'magic' of hypnotism. If you are not on guard against your own unconscious motivations, you can end up in a pretty bad situation.

Easy Success

Easy success in hypnotizing others is a subtle danger for the amateur or stage hypnotist who tends to work only with the very easy deep trance subjects. If you only work with easy subjects who provide easy successes, you tend to over-emphasize the bizarre phenomena which may occur in deep trances to the exclusion of a broader understanding of the whole science. Working only with easy subjects gives you a restricted concept of hypnosis itself; you will not study the very practical aspects of light trances. I suppose there is no greater danger to us as students of hypnotism than to experience a kind of self-hypnotic euphoria which you get when you fall under this spell (the illusion that you have such compelling power over a subject). Even if we try to dignify this idea that we possess some magical power as something definable, demonstrable, and our unique gift, it is self-deception. This delusion of grandeur carries with it the seeds of destruction. The stage hypnotist cultivates it because it is necessary for his performance (and it is often characteristic of entertainers in general), but I think this delusion of grandeur is a characteristic of charlatans of all kinds.

Sincerity and Empathy

There are problems which may arise for the sensitive and empathetic hypnotherapist as well. If he is not careful, he can become almost sick with the sickness of others. He may over-identify with a patient to the point where he is not only elated when he is successful, but may feel too easily crushed by defeat. This is a danger inherent in all the caring professions: clinicians, doctors, counsellors, psychotherapists, ministers and indeed all who really care deeply about the people they try to help. People in the caring professions must have proper training to help them deal with those feelings.

5.

The Laws of Suggestion

When you understand the laws of suggestion you will know all there really is to know about the principles behind all hypnotic inductions and susceptibility tests. It is not a mere figure of speech to refer to the 'laws' of suggestion. They are scientific principles which govern suggestibility.

The laws of suggestion were formulated from the teachings of Emile Coué. You will remember that the history of hypnotism began with the idea of power residing in the hypnotist. This was conceived of as a sort of physical force similar to magnetism. But even in Mesmer's time there was the Portuguese monk, Abbé Faria, who said, 'No, it has more to do with concentration than anything else'. It was soon understood that hypnosis was a psychological phenomenon rather than a purely physical one.

When Braid started his 'fascination' or 'eye-fixation' period, the idea was to concentrate the gaze of the person. He soon realized it was a matter of concentrating the attention rather than merely the gaze. Then the next step in the development of understanding hypnotic phenomena lay in the contributions of Emile Coué, the French pharmacist who began to focus on the laws of suggestion. Coué's method, basically, was to use the phrase, 'Every day in every way, I'm getting better and better.' Coué felt that you did not really need to be too specific for the subconscious mind because it has a wisdom of its own and knows what you need, perhaps better than you do. He felt that a general, completely positive, suggestion would be interpreted by each individual's subconscious according to his particular inner needs.

One method that Coué recommended to the people in France at that time was to tie twenty knots in a length of ordinary string, so a person could count with a minimum expenditure of conscious attention. (As a devout Catholic counts his prayers on a rosary, Coué adapted his method to the customs of the people he worked with.) The number twenty had no intrinsic value but was simply adopted as a suitable round number.

Here is Coué's advice: on getting into bed, close your eyes, relax your muscles, and take a comfortable position. (These are no more than the ordinary preliminaries of going to sleep.) Then repeat twenty times, counting by means of the knotted string, the general formula, 'Every day in every way, I'm getting better and better'. The words should be uttered loud enough to be audible to your own ears so that the idea is reinforced by the movements of lips and tongue and by the auditory impressions through the ear. This is to be effortless, as a child absently murmurs a nursery rhyme. Thus you avoid a critical appeal to the faculties of the conscious mind, which would lessen the results. Today we would call it 'by-passing the critical faculty'.

When you have got used to this exercise and can say it quite unselfconsciously (not 'unconsciously', but simply 'unselfconsciously' — a good expression), begin to let your voice rise or fall (it does not matter which) on the phrase 'in every way' with a gentle emphasis, which is perhaps the most important part of the formula. To attempt this emphasis at first would only needlessly complicate things by requiring more conscious attention, which may introduce effort. Do not try to think of what you are saying. On the contrary, let your mind wander at will. If it rests on the formula, all the better. If it strays elsewhere, do not recall it. As long as the repetition does not come to a full stop, your mind wandering will be less disturbing than would be the effort to recall your thought. But keep repeating the formula.

Coué had a disciple named Charles Baudouin, who wrote *Suggestion and Autosuggestion*, which in my opinion is the best book on the subject ever written. (Nothing written since has improved on it in any way.) Baudouin differed from Coué in that he suggested that you say the formula 'piously', with all the words separately stressed. No doubt it has value when spoken that way, but the attitude of mind to which 'pious' can be applied is unfortunately not habitual with everyone; the average man, in trying to be pious, might end up merely being artificial. However, because the child still exists in the most mature adult, Coué considered that this simple method was the best.

Coué's Clinic

It seems that books by or about Coué are very rare. One good book is *Better and Better Every Day*, (which is actually two books in one, *Self-Mastery Through Conscious AutoSuggestion*, by Emile Coué, and *The Practice of Autosuggestion by the Method of Emile Coué*, by C. H. Brooks).

As his fame spread, so many people sought Coué's aid that he developed a method of individualized treatment even while dealing with sizeable groups. Coué lived at the end of a secluded street, in a large house with several buildings and a garden, and it was from this ideal setting that he conducted his clinical work.

Because of his unique ability to have a suggested healing influence on groups, it is easy to compare him with 'faith healers', but Coué would not be flattered by the comparison, for the only thing that religious healers have in common with him is that they may inadvertently utilize the principles of hypnotic suggestion. Coué employed scientific laws he had discovered; he never made appeal to anyone's religious beliefs.

C. H. Brooks visited one of Coué's famous group therapy sessions at his home in 1921 and gave an eye-witness account of the 'master' at work. He described how little groups of patients sat on the garden seats or strolled among the fruit trees, while others sat in a one-floor construction which served as a waiting room. In the two-floor building which served as the clinic, some patients sat on folding chairs, others sat on the floor or in a window-seat, while yet more crowded the doorway. Brooks described how Coué found a seat for him with some difficulty and immediately began his treatments.

Coué first addressed a frail, middle-aged man with a cane who had come from Paris to consult him, accompanied by his young daughter. The man walked with difficulty and his head, arms and legs were afflicted by a continual tremor. He described how, when a stranger noticed his affliction while walking in the street, he would become paralysed and had to hold any available support to keep from falling. Coué required him to demonstrate, and the man leaned on his cane and walked with half-bent legs, dragging his feet heavily. Coué promised him improvement, adding, 'You have been sowing bad seed in your Unconscious, but now you will sow good seed. The power by which you have produced these ill effects will in the future produce equally good ones.' This was his essential message to all the patients in the room.

When one woman began to complain of her many ailments in voluble detail, he cut her short, reminding her that she thought too much about her problems and in doing so created fresh ones. He spoke with others about their headaches, rheumatism, paralytic afflictions, nervousness, lack of self-confidence, and haunting fears. He explained how their efforts to rid themselves of negative thoughts only fatigued them further. 'If you say,' he told them, "I want to do something," your imagination replies, "Oh, but you can't." You must say, "I am going to do it," and if it is in the region of the possible you will succeed.'

Many of those present testified that they had already improved by following his advice. To one patient who reported no progress at all, he chided, 'Monsieur, you have been making efforts. You must put your trust in the imagination, not in the will. Think you are better and you will become so.' Several who could not walk without support were asked to demonstrate their condition as a criterion against which to measure their future progress. A former blacksmith complained that for ten years he had not been able to lift his right arm above shoulder level. For forty minutes Coué continued this personalized approach, emphasizing that autosuggestion, if conscientiously applied, could either cure them or retard the progress of their afflictions. For those with advanced organic diseases, he promised at least a cessation of pain and an improvement of morale. He never rejected the possibility of complete cure, adding, 'The limits of the power of autosuggestion are not yet known. Therefore, final recovery is possible.' None of these remarks constituted suggestion as Coué understood it, but merely his sober opinions which were based on years of experience.

Coué outlined the main conclusions of his theory:

1. Every idea which exclusively occupies the mind is transformed into an actual physical or mental state.
2. The efforts we make to conquer an idea by exerting the will only serve to make that idea more powerful.

To demonstrate this, he conducted an experiment known among hypnotists as the 'hand-clasp suggestibility test' on a volunteer. He asked a woman to extend her arms, her hands clasped firmly with the fingers interlaced, until a slight tremor set in. 'Look at your hands,' he instructed, 'and think that you would like to open them but that you cannot. Now try to pull them apart. Pull hard. You find that the more you try, the more tightly they become clasped together.' The woman's knuckles turned white with the effort and her hands seemed locked by a force beyond her control. 'Now think,' he said,

' "I can open my hands." ' Her hand relaxed and she easily pulled the cramped fingers apart.

Each patient in turn was required to perform the same experiment, and most were successful. One woman sat with her face puckered up and stared at her locked hands. 'If Madame persists in her present idea,' Coué joked, 'she will never open her hands again as long as she lives.' Some of the men, including the blacksmith, easily opened their hands. (At this point, many modern hypnotists would dismiss him as a 'poor subject', but Coué was not an ordinary hypnotist!)

Coué merely smiled. 'You see, it depends not on what I say but on what you think. What were you thinking then?'

'I thought perhaps I could open them after all,' the man admitted.

'Exactly. And therefore you could. Now clasp your hands together.' Coué worked with the man until he could not release the suggested contraction.

'Now listen to me,' Coué said intently. 'For ten years you have been thinking you could not lift your arm above your shoulder, consequently you have not been able to do so, for whatever we think becomes true for us. Now think: "I can lift it." ' The blacksmith looked at him doubtfully. 'Quick!' Coué commanded. 'Think "I can, I can!" ' 'I can,' said the man, making a half-hearted attempt. He complained of a pain in his shoulder. (Here again, most hypnotists would throw up their hands in defeat. But Coué was a master in the art of suggestion.)

'Good,' he said. 'Don't lower your arm. Close your eyes and repeat after me as fast as you can: "It is passing, it is passing." ' They repeated the phrase together for half a minute, as Coué quickly stroked the man's shoulder. The patient admitted the pain was gone. 'Now think well that you can lift your arm,' Coué said softly. The man's face brightened as the power of the suggestion took hold, strengthened by the cessation of pain. 'I can,' he said emphatically, and without effort lifted his arm calmly to its full height above his head, holding it triumphantly as the crowd applauded.

Coué shook his hand and announced, 'My friend, you are cured.' The man said he thought he was, and Coué said, 'Prove it. Hit me on the shoulder.' The man laughingly hit him gently. 'Harder,' encouraged Coué, 'Hit me as hard as you can.' The man did as he was told, until Coué winced at the force of his blows. 'Very well, my friend,' he said. 'Now you can go back to your anvil!' Throughout the remainder of the session, the blacksmith sat in amazement at what had occurred. From time to time he raised his arm as if to reassure himself, whispering in an awed tone, 'I can. I can.'

After each patient had successfully performed the hand-clasp experiment, and Coué had removed their pain by the same method he had used with the blacksmith, he proudly announced, 'Now you are cultivated ground and I can throw out the seed in handfuls.'

He returned to the man from Paris who could not walk without support, and made him stand and place his weight on each foot in turn, doing the exercise known as 'marking time' or 'walking in place'. Then Coué took away his cane and made him walk back and forth, constantly thinking 'I can'. When the man faltered, Coué stopped him, pointed out the failure to keep thinking 'I can', and encouraged him to continue. The man's little daughter danced for joy as his bearing became more erect and confident under Coué's encouragement, and the crowd clapped their hands. 'After the sitting,' Coué announced, 'you shall come for a run in my garden!'

Coué then asked them to close their eyes as he began in a monotonous voice to evoke before their minds powerful suggestions of health and well-being. Then he gave particular suggestions to each sufferer. When the session was finished, he instructed them to follow the practice of daily autosuggestion, using the phrase 'Every day, in every way, I am getting better and better.'

When we consider the near-miraculous transformation of the blacksmith and the cripple from Paris, as well as many others, it would be easy to understand how Coué's patients might look upon him with reverence. However, Coué concluded by explaining that he possessed no healing power and had never healed anyone in his life: they carried within themselves the healing power of their own positive thoughts, and henceforth they could, and must, forge their own destinies.

At the end of the session, many crowded around Coué to declare that they were either cured or much improved, but he waved them aside and took the three patients who could not walk (including the man from Paris) to a gravel path in the garden. He encouraged them to walk without support, reinforcing the thoughts of strength and power. Then he asked them to run!

Eye-witness C. H. Brooks reported that,

> They started rather uncertainly, but Coué followed them with persistent encouragements. They began to raise their heads, to lift their feet from the ground and run with greater freedom and confidence. Turning at the end of the path they came back at a fair pace. Their movements were not elegant, but people

on the farther side of fifty are rarely elegant runners. It was a surprising sight to see these sufferers who had hobbled to the clinic on sticks now covering the ground at a full five miles an hour, and laughing heartily at themselves as they ran. The crowd of patients who had collected broke into a spontaneous cheer, and Coué, slipping modestly away, returned to the fresh company of sufferers who awaited him within.

This account has far more than mere historical interest. To be sure, we can see the similarity of Coué's technique with what we refer to as mass healing meetings, but the story is filled with information for the serious student of hypnosis. It would indeed be interesting to see what a man like Coué would do with a group of sick people in a modern clinic. According to Brooks,

> Coué's manner was always quietly inspiring. There was no formality, no attitude of the superior person; he treated everyone, whether rich or poor, with the same friendly solicitude. But within these limits he varied his tone to suit the temperament of the patient. Sometimes he was firm, sometimes gently bantering. He seized every opportunity for a little humorous by-play. One might almost say that he tactfully teased some of his patients, giving them an idea that their ailment was absurd, and a little unworthy; that to be ill was a quaint but reprehensible weakness, which they should quickly get rid of. Indeed, this denial of the dignity of disease is one of the characteristics of the place. No homage is paid to it as a Dread Monarch. It is gently ridiculed, its terrors are made to appear second-rate, and its victims end by laughing at it.

You might conclude that, 'All those people just had psychosomatic illnesses or hysterical symptoms; they were just a bunch of neurotics and it was all in their heads.' Coué might have replied. 'Yes, possibly. That's just the whole point. That's why they didn't get cured by pills and potions and so forth. Of course it's all in their minds.'

Abbé Faria had said, 'A person can be charmed into sickness, and can be charmed into health.' In Coué's terms, the patients had been suggested into it,and they could be suggested out of it.

The Three Laws of Suggestion

The laws of suggestion are far from being complicated. In fact, they are simple. For many years people flocked to Coué's free clinic in north east France and numerous remarkable cures took place. Although he is only remembered for his little phrase, 'Every day in every way, I'm getting better and better', this is obviously an over-simplification of his great work. It is basically a misunderstanding which was caused by the American press when he came to the United States. They made light of his system and over-simplified it, misunderstanding it. In spite of that, the fact is (in my opinion at least, and shared by many knowledgeable hypnotists) that Coué was a genius. He was a man of heroic stature in the history of suggestive therapeutics.

Charles Baudouin was a disciple of Coué and he put all this into a system. Coué was not much of a writer or a philosopher; his mind did not run along those lines at all. So it was up to Baudouin to systematize Coué's thoughts for him. The laws of suggestion are Coué's, but they are now known in the form that Charles Baudouin finally put them. He said that there were three laws of suggestion and these three laws explain everything that occurs through suggestion. These are the three laws:

1. *The Law of Concentrated Attention*
The law of concentrated attention means that when a person concentrates his attention on an idea, that idea tends to realize itself.
2. *The Law of Reverse Effort*
This means that when a person thinks he cannot do something and then tries, the more he tries to do it the less able he is to do it.
3. *The Law of Dominant Affect*
This means that a suggestion linked to an emotion will surmount any other suggestion in the mind at the time. The dominating affect (emotion) connected to that suggestion causes it to have a stronger influence on the mind.

Coué said, 'Thus understood, autosuggestion is nothing but hypnotism, as I see it, and I would define it in these simple words: the influence of the imagination upon the moral and physical being of mankind.'

Properly understood, hypnotism has absolutely nothing to do with 'will power'. Will power (or 'won't power', as the case may be) is a function of the conscious mind, whereas the subconscious mind is basically influenced by the imagination. In any battle between the imagination and the will power, it is the imagination that invariably wins, despite the protestations of most people.

Regarding this, Coué made the following observations based on his personal daily experience over a period of twenty years' practice:

1. When the will and the imagination are antagonistic, it is always the imagination which wins, *without exception*!
2. In the conflict between the will and the imagination, the force of the imagination is in direct ratio to the square of the will.
3. When the will and the imagination are in agreement, one does not add to the other, but one is multiplied by the other.
4. The imagination can be directed.

Walking the Plank

Now, the classic example of all this would be if we had a six-inch plank stretched the length of a building and I asked, 'Can you walk this plank from one end to the other without falling off?'

You would say, 'What do you mean, could I do it without falling off?'

'Well, it's six inches wide. Can you walk along the entire length of it without stepping off on the floor; can you stay on the board?'

You would say, 'Certainly, I can do that. Anybody can do that.'

I'd say, 'Well, fine. If we put this board up on two stools, or up between two tables about three feet above the floor, could you walk across it without falling?' You would probably agree still.

Then if I would say, 'Well, that's wonderful! We've taken out advertisements in the paper, put up posters, sold lots of tickets, and tomorrow at noon we will have this plank stretched from one building to another, about a hundred feet off the ground, and we've been looking for someone who would volunteer to walk that plank for us. We're so glad you volunteered!'

I am sure you would protest, 'Wait a minute! Hold everything! I'm not about to get up a hundred feet off the ground and walk a six-inch plank!'

I think everyone would react that way — I know I would. While waiting for the lift on the tenth floor of a building once, pacing up and down the corridor, I noticed the square floor tiles. I looked out of the window at the end of the corridor and thought, 'If I can walk on this twelve-inch tile, why couldn't I walk a twelve-inch plank over to the next building?' I looked out of the window ten storeys down and I tell you, there is not enough money in the world to get me to even attempt such a thing! Now, why is this?

Logically, there is no reason why anybody cannot do that. If you can walk a plank when it is on the floor, you should also be able to do it a hundred feet in the air. Why can't you logically do that? What's the difference? The difference is, you shake your head and think, 'I *can't* do that!'

Coué would explain it like this: the Law of Concentrated Attention means that when a person concentrates his attention on an idea, it tends to realize itself. Now, if you concentrate on the idea (imagine) that you are going to fall, there is a tendency for that idea to realize itself — you fall! You see, this is very simple. This law can be demonstrated on the stage or in a class; we call it the 'falling back' susceptibility test. If you have an idea in your mind and your attention is concentrated on that idea, then that idea tends to express itself and be realized in actual experience.

The next law that comes into the picture is Coué's third law, the Law of Dominant Affect. This means that when a suggestion (falling) becomes linked to an emotion (fear) it makes that idea the dominant one in your mind, counteracting or expelling all others. So, the emotion of fear enters into the simple idea of falling and it then becomes the *fear of falling*. This combination of emotion plus suggestion (the imagined idea of falling) makes it all-powerful at the moment.

The Law of Reverse Effort, Coué's second law of suggestion, is also illustrated in this example. That law says that if you think you cannot do something, then the harder you try the less able you are to do it. So, since you *know* (believe or imagine) you *can't* get from here to there without falling off the plank, according to this law of suggestion, you can't *no matter how hard you try*!

Let us now analyse Coué's observations on the will and the imagination, to be sure we understand it. When the will and the imagination are antagonistic or in conflict, the imagination always wins. That is the first principle.

Secondly, if the imagination and the will are in a conflict, then the force of the imagination is equal to the square of the power of the will. In other words, the more force the will exerts (the harder you try), that much power is squared; there is still more than enough power from the imagination to counteract it, according to the first principle. Remember, this is when the will and the imagination *are in conflict*. As long as they are in conflict, you *can't* ever have enough will power because the more will power you exert, the more power that gives the imagination to overcome it.

Now then, Coué says that when the will and the imagination are *in agreement* (as they should be in autosuggestion), the power that results is not merely the power of the one plus the other one, but it is the force of the one *multiplied* by the other one. If you can get your imagination hooked up and geared to your will power, you have multiplied both of these forces in your mental life.

Coué's last point is that the imagination *can* be directed. In other words, this is not just something about which to say, 'Well, that's interesting, but what can I do about it?' He says you can *direct* this imagination for your benefit.

Memorize the names of these laws and I think you will understand them. The Law of Concentrated Attention means that when the attention is concentrated on an idea it tends to become manifested. The Law of Reverse Effort means that as long as you believe you cannot do something, the harder you try the less able you will be to do it. Lastly, the Law of Dominant Affect means that when a suggestion is linked to an emotion, then it supersedes any other suggestion which might be in the mind at that time.

Susceptibility Tests

You have probably seen or read about susceptibility tests in hypnosis. These tests are supposed to be measures of a person's susceptibility to suggestion and therefore their suitability as a hypnotic subject. Actually, when you analyse it, these tests or stunts are measures of a person's imagination. They measure susceptibility by measuring the imagination with a little experiment. A person who can readily visualize and mentally participate in any suggested situation is a good hypnotic subject. This is not pretence in the sense that you pretend something that is not so, but rather like the games you played as a child when you said, 'Let's play like . . .' When you do that, it evokes the emotional response that approximates what would happen if the imagined experience were in fact real.

It is a theory in dramatics, isn't it? You 'live' the role. You 'put yourself into it' and imagine, 'What would I feel like if, in fact, I were this person, in this circumstance, etc.?' If you can visualize that situation and see yourself in it and identify with it, then you evoke the emotional and physical responses which you would have if what you imagined were real.

This is valuable knowledge for those engaged in hypnosis or self-hypnosis for self-improvement. If you can 'plan your work and work your plan' according to these scientific laws of suggestion, you cannot help but be successful in any effort involving the 'power of suggestion'.

6.

Questions and Answers

What is hypnotism?

Hypnotism is the science of influencing the perceptions and behaviour of others by means of two factors: the laws of suggestion, and the state known as hypnotic 'trance'.

Three words should be distinguished from each other: hypnotism, hypnosis and hypnology. 'Hypnotism' refers to the *methods*, known as 'induction techniques', of achieving hypnotic phenomena. 'Hypnosis' is the mind-body *state* produced by a temporary modification of the nervous system as a result of the induction technique. 'Hypnology' is the overall term which refers to the *science* of understanding the nature and utility of all hypnotic states, hypnotic phenomena and induction methods.

The state of hypnosis, brought about by hypnotism, is characterized by a by-pass of the critical faculties, plus selective thinking or suggestion. It is both a restricted awareness (that is, ignoring distractions) and an increased concentration on those ideas to which the attention is drawn by the hypnotist. In short, hypnotism produces the increased ability to concentrate effortlessly as directed.

What is a 'hypnotic' trance?

A 'trance' is a mind-body condition of a temporary neurological modification, brought about by stimulation of either the sympathetic or parasympathetic nervous system.

A trance is *not* a state of either 'coma', 'sleep' or 'unconsciousness'. It is neither a fully conscious state nor an unconscious one, but can best be described as 'off-conscious'. These 'off-conscious' states result in increased suggestibility. Such states can be produced in many ways, such as by disease, by drugs or by suggestion.

A trance, because it is a condition resulting from a greater than usual stimulation of the nervous system, should be understood as basically a physical condition. In hypnotism, this is brought about by the intensification of emotions of either the disturbing or comforting kinds, by means of suggestions. Therefore there are two basic types of trance possible, depending on which type of emotion is stimulated.

A 'hypnotic trance' is a trance brought on by one of the various inter-personal methods known as hypnotic inductions. In short, a trance produced by suggestion is called a 'hypnotic' trance. The most common type of hypnotic trance, or off-conscious state of awareness, is induced by the hypnotist giving suggestions to intensify the comforting emotions.

A number of physiological changes takes place when a person experiences a hypnotic trance. These changes vary according to whether the hypnotist has given suggestions to intensify disturbing or comforting emotions.

Are all trances essentially the same?

The word 'trance' is frequently mis-used to apply to states of semi-consciousness, or mere dazed and stuporous conditions. These popular and metaphorical ways of using the word have no scientific meaning.

The trance is actually a neurological phenomenon. If it is the result of stimulation of the sympathetic nervous system, by means of intensifying disturbing emotions, it is called an 'ergotropic' trance. If it is the result of stimulation of the parasympathetic nervous system, by means of intensifying comforting emotions, it is called a 'trophotropic' trance. These two types of hypnotic trances are sometimes referred to by hypnotists as 'negative' and 'positive' trances, respectively.

A person may be frightened or 'worked-up' into a negative trance, which is the type brought on by voodoo drums, traumatic experiences, etc. Such negative trances are often characterized by frenzied body movements and mental disorganization of an extreme type.

On the other hand, the positive trance is a comfortable and relaxed state. A person is soothed and lulled into it. It is this positive trance which is used almost exclusively by modern hypnotherapists for beneficial purposes.

All negative trances are qualitatively the same; all positive trances are qualitatively the same. The same distinct physiological and psychological characteristics are present in each type (although each type is distinct from the other) whether these states are produced by accident, by ritual, by self-direction or by another person. However, only when they are scientifically produced by hypnological methods can they appropriately be called 'hypnotic trances'.

Is the state of 'trance' harmful in any way?

This naturally depends on which type of trance is under consideration. The negative trance is a state of sympathetic nervous system 'shock'. It is basically a condition in which the nervous system has been stimulated to 'fight or flight' and then not permitted to do either. In a mild form, it could feel exciting and exhilarating. In an extreme form, it would be frightening and border on panic.

The negative trance is therefore a temporary but intense manifestation of what otherwise has been called the 'stress syndrome', which can have very harmful psychosomatic effects. Since it is analogous to being frightened out of one's wits, it certainly could be dangerous to persons of unstable nervous temperaments, weakened physical condition, etc.

On the other hand, the positive trance is a profoundly relaxed state caused by stimulation of the parasympathetic nervous system, and therefore results in a condition of inner tranquillity, balance and harmony. It is a mind-body state in which disturbing factors are at a minimum and the body's restorative and recuperative powers are at a maximum or optimum level. It is the ultimate type of 'rest cure'. There are no medical contraindications to the positive trance.

It must also be remembered that all trance states, of whichever type and however they may be induced, are completely temporary in nature. The body cannot support either extreme indefinitely, but will eventually normalize itself.

What are the proofs of a trance state?

Although it is easy for a person to act as if they were hypnotized in a way which will fool most people, it is impossible to deceive an expert hypnotist. There are signs and indications of the trance state which cannot be faked, because they are involuntary results of the stimulation of the nervous system.

Most experienced hypnotists can spot an authentic hypnotic trance by mere observation. Scientific hypnotists note the following signs of the positive trance: increased body warmth, increased lacrimation, increased salivation, upturned eyeballs or slow uncoordinated eye movements (under closed eyelids), and a slight redness of the whites of the eyes right after opening them. Immobility is also a sign of the positive trance; it is caused by a diminished 'annoyance reflex' which can be specifically tested for by determining the absence of the eyelash or eyelid reflex.

Response to the suggestions given is not always a reliable test of the positive trance, because most of the hypnotist's 'challenges' can be faked. Unless the response to suggestions is obviously involuntary, it cannot be used to determine the existence of the trance state *per se*. However, a hypnotized person responds to suggestions in a characteristic way known as 'trance logic', and this can be helpful to a hypnotist in determining a true trance state.

Of what practical use is the trance?

The positive 'trophotropic' trance, produced by the stimulation of the parasympathetic nervous system by the intensifying of comforting emotions, is definitely of therapeutic value whether or not any suggestions are given!

However, the main value of the hypnotic trance is that it either causes, or co-exists with, a state of increased selective awareness and suggestibility. Therefore, it can be used to implant helpful, healthful suggestions into the subconscious. The trance state of awareness opens up a channel, as it were, into the subconscious, allowing positive thoughts to be implanted deeply in the mind. This 'open channel' to the subconscious can also work in reverse. It can be utilized to discover and extract deeply repressed material from the subconscious.

The practical uses of the trance state could be 'applied to any activity of the human mind, whether the objective was to put something in or take something out. Obviously, any method which makes accessible for therapeutic purposes that which is normally inaccessible to the mind will not only benefit in treatments, but will also greatly increase our understanding of the inner workings of the human mind. This knowledge can immeasurably increase our utilization of normally hidden and otherwise incomprehensible powers.

As a mode of studying the nature of the human mind itself — its perceptions, comprehensions, levels of consciousness, etc. — as well as for therapeutic and self-improvement purposes, it should be obvious that the positive trance is one of the most useful and practical phenomena known to mankind.

Are there 'superhuman' powers inherent in the trance?

No. But because hypnotic trance phenomena may sometimes appear mysterious, it may be easy for some people mistakenly to attribute some superhuman quality to it. We tend to 'supernaturalize' anything unfamiliar to us or which is not readily explainable in familiar terms.

The average person never has an opportunity to observe hypnotic trance phenomena over any long period of time, in order to familiarize himself with it, and so it forever remains mysterious. It is therefore easy for him, not being familiar with the scientific explanation, to adopt vague and unscientific theories about it.

As our understanding of hypnological science increases, all hypnotic phenomena will become quite explainable in more familiar terms. As the public becomes more enlightened and the benefits of hypnosis are made more accessible, its very commonness will tend to diminish and dispel its present 'mystique'.

It is true that in the hypnotic trance some people frequently seem to transcend their normal abilities. However, since all psychologists agree that man uses only a very small percentage of his mental powers, we may assume that many innate powers are normally blocked from expression due to psychological problems, or simply because they are unknown or unrecognized by the individual.

Sometimes a person's usual level of achievement is extended through hypnosis and feats are accomplished which would lead the naïve observer to conclude there was something 'superhuman' about it. But, of course, anything a human can do is not, strictly speaking, superhuman, no matter how unusual it may be.

How did man discover hypnotism?

Although there is much that we do not know about the origins of hypnotism, we do know that its use is very ancient. In some ancient writings, clay tablets, cave drawings, etc., there are obvious references to practices which today we would consider to be forms of hypnotism.

The knowledge of hypnotism throughout the ages advanced both by accident and design. Like much of man's primitive science which began by accident, the phenomenon of trance was observed to occur accidentally or unintentionally under given circumstances. At first these trances were probably of the negative type, caused by fear reactions in battle or daily life.

Certain men (the priests, shamans, medicine-men, etc.) found that by duplicating certain stimuli of the original trance-evoking experience, they could thereby induce a trance artificially. These methods became ritualized through trial-and-error. They worked most of the time, but no one knew exactly why. After many centuries of inducing trances in this way, it was discovered how to induce trances of the positive type as well. Because the effects of this type of hypnotism were more beneficial, physicians and true scientists became interested in it.

A few progressive thinkers and careful observers were able, over the centuries, to analyse the precise reasons which made various induction methods successful. As time went on, it became possible to eliminate some of the non-essential 'trappings' of earlier methods and to isolate and refine the essential factors in the techniques. This constant improvement in methodology continues today and no doubt will continue in the future.

Can everyone be hypnotized?

Until recently it was believed that only certain people could be hypnotized. This conclusion was based on the old cumbersome hit-or-miss methods of hypnotism formerly used, and upon the later practice of stage hypnotists to eliminate quickly the difficult subjects and use the easy ones. This gave the impression that there were either 'good' or 'bad' subjects for hypnotism.

As long as hypnotism proceeded along these lines, it naturally led to the supposition that unless certain spectacular responses by the subject were immediately obtainable, little or no degree of hypnosis was present. This attitude led to a very narrow understanding of hypnotism.

More modern advances in our knowledge of hypnology have produced different conclusions. As induction techniques were refined and diversified it was found that practically everyone can be hypnotized, providing they have either the need or the desire.

Sometimes, even when it is impossible to induce the trance by verbal means, non-verbal methods have been developed so that deaf-mutes and even the mentally retarded can now be hypnotized. While it is not always possible to 'suggest' much in the conventional sense, the therapeutic value is not lost entirely.

Modern research in hypnotism has cast aside many of the old assumptions and this is especially true regarding the antiquated ideas about hypnotizability.

Can anyone become a hypnotist?

Since hypnotism is a science it would be reasonable to assume that anyone could acquire the knowledge and experience to become a hypnotist. But because modern clinical hypnotism requires unusual skill in interpersonal communication, it is obvious that not everyone is temperamentally suited for it.

Just as anyone can be hypnotized by someone, certainly anyone can learn to hypnotize someone. In this sense, 'anyone' can become a 'hypnotist'. However, in any professional or practical sense, it requires much more than an elementary or superficial know-how.

In the past, successful hypnotists were individuals who just naturally possessed certain personality traits which inspired either confidence, awe or submission in others. These people managed to learn certain limited techniques whereby they could hypnotize carefully selected subjects. By using various subtle (and some not so subtle) 'tests' they could pick out the most susceptible subjects from a group and disregard the rest. This made them highly successful in hypnotizing a small percentage of people, relatively unsuccessful with a vast majority, and completely ineffective with a few.

Modern hypnological science does not rely so much on the elements of 'prestige suggestion' as did the older, more authoritarian methods of trance induction. To be able to hypnotize successfully more than ninety per cent of people (not just a few selected from a group of volunteers) requires a great deal of knowledge and experience, plus the ability to establish an immediate 'rapport', or a sense of confidence and mutual acceptance.

How many methods are there for hypnotism?

There are two basic methods. One is induction of the negative or ergotropic trance by stimulating what is called the 'stress syndrome'. This can be done in many ways, but all are very stimulating and may have harmful psychosomatic effects.

The other basic method, more popular today, is the positive trance induction by stimulating the parasympathetic nervous system. This produces a profoundly relaxed state which results in a condition of inner tranquillity, balance and harmony.

Within the confines of these two basic approaches, the actual content of the induction method is limited only by the hypnotist's imagination. A hundred methods have probably been devised, but a dozen or so have become standardized in actual practice. It must be remembered that all trance states produced by either of the two basic methods (called 'authoritarian' in the first method, and 'permissive' in the second, or any variation of these) are temporary in nature. The body cannot support either extreme indefinitely, but will eventually normalize itself.

During the past two hundred years there have been several schools of thought regarding hypnotism. Each looked at the phenomenon from a different point of view and thus developed a different theory. This led them to devise induction methods which seemed consistent with those theories. Many old *theories* have been disproven or discarded with the passing of time, but the two basic *methods* of hypnotizing still work. However, as far as the specific contents of various induction methods are concerned, it can truly be said that if one has the modern knowledge, 'There just isn't any way you *can't* hypnotize a person!'

What does 'animal magnetism' mean and what is its relation to hypnotism?

Animal magnetism is the name of one of the disproven and discarded theories used to explain hypnotic phenomena in terms of a 'magnetic' force within the body. At one time it was popular to induce the trance by various 'passes' or stroking movements over the head and body of the subject, either with or without contact. Assuming hypnotic phenomena to be 'magnetic' in nature, the method of making passes was believed to alter or control the 'flow of magnetism' from the hypnotist to the subject.

When the theory of 'animal magnetism' was discredited, it became known as 'Mesmerism' after its founder, Franz Anton Mesmer, who had popularized it in the 1770s. Even after it was discredited in Europe, it spread to America in the 1850s and became a common theme in the entertainment media, thereby greatly influencing the public's ideas of hypnotism. Mesmeric experiments were the basis of DuMaurier's *Trilby* and Edgar Allen Poe's *The Strange Facts in the Case of* M. *Valdemar.*

The word 'hypnotism' was coined by James Braid in the mid-1800s to avoid the stigma which had become associated with the terms 'animal magnetism' or 'Mesmerism'. Actually, the word 'hypnotism' was based on the false idea that the phenomenon was a special form of sleep. (The Greek word 'hypnos' means 'sleep'.) But it was soon discovered that hypnotism had as little to do with sleep as it did with magnetism.

Although both Mesmer and Braid were mistaken about the nature of hypnotism, their methods ('passes', staring at a bright light, etc.) are still effective even though most hypnotists now consider them to be cumbersome, awkward and obsolete.

Is there any truth in 'animal magnetism' or 'Mesmerism'?

Mesmer was a doctor who represented the best in the education and culture of his times. He made remarkable discoveries and pioneered a new area of behavioural science; it is one of the tragedies of history that the men of 'science' in his day ridiculed him until they had practically buried the subject. Mesmer's theories were discredited simply because there was no evidence that 'animal magnetism' existed.

Although his theories of 'magnetism' were false, certainly the results produced by Mesmer's method were factual and worthy of scientific study. The fact that the methods as well as the theory were made objects of derision probably set the science of true hypnotism back at least a hundred years.

Mesmer's methods of trance induction are virtually unused today because faster and more efficient ways have been discovered. 'Magnetic' theories and their counterparts, the 'emanation' theories, have been unfruitful for experimentation. We now understand the psychological aspects of hypnotism and recognize the 'passes' as forms of non-verbal suggestion.

To the extent that the Mesmerists' observations were accurately recorded, there is some 'truth' to them, of course. Likewise, to the extent that they were effective, we can admit there is some 'truth' in the methods. However, Mesmerism was inadequate and misleading as a theory to advance our scientific understanding of hypnotic phenomena, and therefore in that sense 'untrue'.

Isn't hypnotism just a matter of suggestion?

It should be kept in mind that 'suggestion' is simply one of the theories advanced to explain hypnosis. Perhaps we should be cautious about assuming that hypnotism is 'just' a matter of suggestion until we have a broader understanding of 'suggestion'.

In research in the United States, most respected researchers have focused their attention on the 'suggestion' aspect of hypnosis, while those in other countries conduct research into (assumed) non-suggestive aspects of hypnosis. Therefore, to speak of hypnosis solely from the standpoint of 'suggestion' may force a too restrictive view of the matter. Suggestion might be only a small part of a more complex process in the phenomena of hypnosis.

It seems that hypnosis is a mind-body state which increases one's awareness and suggestibility, and the fact that it is often induced by suggestion may be a historical artifact. In 'animal hypnosis' the trance clearly can be separated from any concept of suggestion.

Hypnosis is a complex phenomenon. It is probably a simplistic mistake to think of it as 'just' any one thing, whatever that might be.

Are there really any 'laws' of suggestion?

Emile Coué and Charles Baudouin developed what are known today as the 'laws of suggestion'. Coué was a French pharmacist who pioneered the theory and practice of the 'placebo effect' until he had developed an effective method of treatment and self-improvement. His work was unfortunately over-simplified and therefore vastly underrated. Coué was more of a practitioner than a theorist and it remained for his disciple, Charles Baudouin, to articulate his teachings in a logical system of 'laws'.

It was found that basically all the effects of suggestion could be summarized into three principles and satisfactorily explained thereby. These three principles have been proven to be so accurate (so valid and reliable) that they can truly be considered 'laws' of suggestion. They are descriptively named the Law of Concentrated Attention, the Law of Dominant Affect and the Law of Reverse Effort.

Yes, indeed there are 'laws' of suggestion, and this is one of the factors which makes hypnotism a science. There no longer need be any guesswork to it if the three laws are followed correctly.

In what sense can hypnotism be called a 'science'?

Hypnotism can be called a science today because it comprises systematized knowledge derived from accurate observation, study and experimentation, carried on in order to determine the nature of the principles involved. Understood in this sense, hypnotism is as much a science as anything else is. It deals with natural phenomena which are subject to well-defined laws or principles. The vast amount of experimentation and research in the field of hypnosis each year is continually increasing the status of hypnosis as a recognized science.

There is a sense, of course, in which hypnotism may be considered an art as well as a science, for in addition to the study and mastery of its principles, it requires practice and experience to be an adept practitioner. In earlier days, hypnotists were more like artists than scientists. They had a talent, a flair, for inducing the hypnotic state which they exercised intuitively without intellectually understanding the reasons for their success. Only in recent years has there been an attempt to analyse the 'art' of hypnotism to the point where it can be understood in terms of natural science and reduced to principles which can be duplicated under experimental conditions.

This understanding of hypnosis can be taught as a science and therefore deserves to be fully treated as such.

If hypnotism is a science, why aren't more scientists working with hypnosis?

Actually, more scientists are working with hypnotism today than at any other time in history! The average person has no conception of the vast amount of experimental and research data on hypnosis that has been amassed over the past twenty years, and continues to increase each year. Also, the average English-speaking hypnotist has little conception of the many exciting developments in hypnology that have been made in other countries.

Hypnotism has always developed in cycles. Enthusiastic and unrestrained revivals of interest have traditionally been followed by periods of disinterest and disuse. When exaggerated claims are made for hypnosis, even by serious practitioners who nonetheless lack a scientific orientation, it unfortunately causes some scientists to treat it as a humbug.

For the past thirty years hypnotism has been in very good hands. Although it still experiences cycles of popularity, it truthfully can be said that there is more solid hypnological work today than ever before.

How can hypnotism be used in medicine?

Hypnotism has already been used extensively in obstetrics, gynaecology, paediatrics, cardiology, surgery, dermatology, psychiatry and dentistry; there have been specialized books on these subjects. A judicious use of hypnosis makes things easier for the doctor as well as the patient, and restores the ideal of the 'bedside manner' to what otherwise may become impersonal medical routine.

Hypnosis is of great advantage in the management of illnesses in which pain is prevalent, constant or intermittent. Its analgesic quality makes it helpful also in painful or uncomfortable examination or treatment procedures. When used as an adjunct to traditional treatment, hypnotic suggestion often has a facilitating or accelerating effect on the desired outcome. Studies on the use of hypnosis to relieve pre- and post-operative anxieties can reduce the time needed for recovery; this makes hypnosis a cost-effective tool in hospital management.

Psychosomatic illnesses are mind-body illnesses in which emotions either cause, aggravate, or sustain the physical symptoms. Hypnosis is a mind-body state in which emotions and ideas can be modified. Hypnotherapy is naturally of great help in the medical treatment and management of this large category of illnesses. Hypnosis may reach its full potential in medicine as soon as medicine better recognizes the scope of psychosomatic disease.

Why don't more doctors use hypnosis?

Most doctors have never been exposed to the therapeutic possibilities of hypnosis because doctors, like everyone else, only know what they have been taught. The teaching of medical hypnosis has been sporadic and inadequate. Therefore, doctors often tend to exhibit the same attitude towards hypnosis as does the uninformed public.

Medical hypnosis has too often been taught superficially and hurriedly in the curriculum, or in three-day 'crash courses' at special seminars or hotel conventions. As a result, some doctors begin using hypnosis only to find that their knowledge is too sketchy to ensure its continued success. After a few failures or disappointing experiences with hypnosis, they discontinue its use, believing it requires too much time to specialize in order to maintain a consistent record of success. Also, they are sometimes discouraged by the crictisms of their uninformed colleagues.

One main reason why hypnosis is not used by more doctors is that they have been exposed only to lengthy, time-consuming induction methods. To be practical for a busy doctor, hypnosis must be almost instantly attainable; this requires the teaching of rapid techniques of hypnotism.

If doctors were more willing to learn from qualified non-medical instructors, there would be no reason why *every* doctor should not advantageously use hypnosis daily.

Should only medical doctors be allowed to practise hypnosis?

While there are a few medical doctors who feel that their profession should control nearly everything and some psychiatrists who feel that they alone of the medical professions should be allowed to practise hypnosis, both are extreme and unwarranted positions.

Certainly it is logical to say that only medical doctors should be allowed to practise *medicine* and that *medical* hypnosis should be performed either by doctors or under their supervision. It ought to be remembered that medical doctors were first taught hypnotism by lay hypnotists and it is safe to say that most qualified instructors of hypnotism today do not have medical degrees.

Hypnosis has too many applications to be artificially restricted to just one profession. In the fields of psychology, education, religion, athletics, business, law enforcement and general self-improvement, hypnosis can be used profitably. If the full potential of hypnosis is to be explored, and eventually utilized for the public good, it will obviously have to be done by people working in those respective fields. Doctors scarcely have time for their medical practices, so to restrict the use of hypnotism to medicine alone would keep the deserving applications of hypnosis in non-medical fields at a standstill for generations to come.

On the other hand, to restrict hypnosis solely to non-clinical applications is completely to misunderstand its essential nature as well.

What other professional groups could use hypnosis to advantage?

Any type of business or profession which deals with the motivations and manipulations of human behaviour, the abilities of the human mind to learn, remember, create or decide, should find the application of the science of hypnosis a helpful ally in the pursuit of success.

In their more 'human' aspects, both business and science could employ hypnological principles to advantage. Professions which are predominantly dependent upon successful interpersonal relationships, such as salesmanship, education, counselling, etc., would naturally find the study of scientific hypnotism of great interest and applicability. Since all such successful activities actually use hypnological principles in a trial-and-error way, it is natural and logical to suppose that a planned, scientific application of the laws of hypnology in a knowledgeable fashion would guarantee further success.

Any activity that involves the human mind has a natural affinity for scientific hypnosis. For this reason, not only the 'professional people' should benefit from hypnosis, but every member of society could profit as well. Certainly every man, woman, and child should want to understand more about the mind and how to direct its energies more scientifically, usefully, and profitably.

How could psychologists use hypnosis?

Psychology is an extensive and complex field: there are separate branches of normal and abnormal psychology, child, adolescent, and adult psychology, animal and human psychology, etc. Each of these branches has its theoretical, experimental and applied aspects. Psychological testing of personality, intelligence and aptitudes has applications in diverse fields such as schools, clinics and industries. New psychological research in perception, motivation, behaviour, and so on, makes the scope of psychology's influence almost endless.

In experimental psychology, hypnosis offers a unique way to study the mind in a controlled fashion. Hypnosis can be adapted to a multitude of experimental designs so that its usefulness is limited only by the imagination and competence of the experimenters. In applied psychology, hypnosis may be used in all forms of psychotherapy as either a diagnostic or therapeutic aid. Hypnosis is compatible with any psychological theory (whether behaviourism, stimulus-response, perceptual, Gestalt, analytic, etc.) so its use is limited only by the therapist. It should be stated that, collectively, psychologists have done more than any other group to stimulate interest in hypnosis.

Isn't it true that psychotics can't be hypnotized at all, and therefore hypnosis is relatively useless in psychiatry?

Psychiatry is the branch of medicine which deals with mental and emotional aberrations of all kinds, not just the psychoses. Psychotics (the medical term designating patients with an extreme illness that the public would term 'crazy' or 'insane') were once assumed to be unsuited for hypnosis, just as for many years they were considered unsuited for medical treatment at all! However, in recent years, some psychiatrists have reported great success using hypnotherapy with selected psychotic patients.

Therefore, it now can be said that many psychotics can be hypnotized and psychiatrists can use hypnotism to understand and treat their conditions. Permissive techniques of hypnotic induction have been refined and diversified to the point where more psychiatrists are finding it a usable and comfortable method with which to work.

Naturally, where the patient's perceptions are unalterably deficient through neurological damage, it can be said that the 'mechanisms of suggestion' are also impaired to the point where verbal aspects of hypnotic suggestion are almost impossible to use. Even in these limited cases, however, non-verbal inductions of hypnotic trance may still be of some help.

What kind of neurotic problems can be helped through hypnosis?

According to the familiar joke, it is neurotics who build castles in the air, psychotics who live in them — and psychiatrists who collect the rent! Neurotics do not suffer from extreme mental illness, but may suffer extreme discomfort and annoyance from their emotional symptoms and maladjustments. Their minor complexes, compulsions, phobias, and fantasies greatly complicate their lives and cause a great deal of mental anguish to themselves and their loved ones.

Provided the patient is able to communicate with the therapist in an articulate and insightful way, hypnosis adds a new dimension to the therapist's method. In general, it is better to say that a patient is treated 'under' rather than 'by' hypnosis. The use of hypnosis enables the therapist to establish better rapport and speed up the treatment process when it is safe to do so.

Since many of the neurotic's problems seem to stem from an

illogical idea deeply rooted on a subconscious level, in a sense many neurotics have been 'hypnotized by events' into expressing neurotic symptoms. Hypnosis provides a clear model whereby the patient can understand just how his symptom was formed, thus giving him insight. Since hypnosis can 'de-hypnotize' him out of a sick idea and 'hypnotize' him into a more healthful one, nearly all kinds of neurotic problems can be helped through hypnosis.

Is it possible to overcome specific fears with hypnosis?

Phobias can take many forms. People are sometimes unreasonably afraid of heights, closed or open spaces, lightning, snakes, insects, etc. There is no limit to the things which can trigger a bizarre fear reaction in some people; it may range from mild discomfort to uncontrollable panic and hysteria. Often the fear is well defined and limited in scope; sometimes it affects many areas of life until the patient is afraid of sickness, death, or even life itself.

Sometimes it is necessary to know exactly what caused the phobia in the first place. Because it has been repressed from consciousness, hypnosis can help in probing for this memory. Usually it is found to consist of more than one specific event and where there is a combination of factors involving a series of unknown events, hypnosis is the best method of uncovering the mystery.

In other cases the cause is known and still the phobia persists. The most promising treatment then seems to be a form of behaviour therapy called 'desensitization', a process in which relaxation and vivid imagery are progressively alternated until the 'hierarchy of fears' become emotionally desensitized. This procedure can be done without hypnosis, but it is greatly facilitated by its use.

What about complexes? Can hypnosis help?

Hypnosis certainly can help in the understanding and treatment of complexes. The amount of help, of course, depends on the nature and severity of the complex. Deep-seated complexes naturally require more intensive help than superficial ones.

However, the most common and bothersome complex is the 'inferiority complex'. Since this is a problem which only 'superior' people have, it easily lends itself to hypnotherapy. (People who actually are inferior, mentally or otherwise, never have a complex about it!) The 'self-concept' of any person can be modified and improved by a combination of success experiences, counselling, intense hypnotic suggestion in vivid detail, and by the use of self-hypnosis or autosuggestion.

The self-concept can be systematically improved; the speed of the process depends on the patient, the possibilities of environmental control during the early treatment, and on the motivation of the patient. This can be done not only by subconsciously indoctrinating him, but also by providing a self-help technique through which he can experience an increasing measure of self-control and confidence.

Self-concept motivates all behaviour, whether normal, deviant, delinquent, or maladaptive conduct. Because hypnosis can directly influence the self-concept, it is obvious that its use logically applies to the treatment of complexes as well as to many other problems.

Is hypnosis of value in treating obesity, alcoholism, smoking or drug-addiction?

Much of the work done with hypnosis in these areas has been of an extremely superficial and limited nature. However, there is sufficient evidence that *whenever and wherever seriously used*, hypnosis has had a dramatic and beneficial effect.

In general, there is a wide range of severity and complexity in these areas; so much so that it often seems a mistake to label a person's problems by those categories. While it is obvious that obesity, alcoholism, smoking and drug-addiction are clinical entities, it is also obvious that not all obese people are fat for the same reason, not all alcoholics drink for the same reason, not all drug addicts take drugs for the same reason, etc. If hypnosis is used in the treatment of these problems, it must take into account these individual differences. Hypnotherapy in these cases must be psychodynamically oriented and not simply an attempt at symptom suppression.

If group hypnotherapy is used, there should be careful sub-grouping to ensure that the treatment is individually adapted to each member of the group. In short. the *person* must be treated, not merely the symptom.

If hypnosis is of value in such cases, why isn't it being widely used?

There are several reasons why hypnosis is not being widely used in these areas. Foremost, of course, is that there are not enough people trained in hypnotherapy.

Alcoholism and drug-addiction are usually treated under institutional, governmental, and quasi-governmental agencies. This involves many reactionary attitudes regarding the illness, the patient, and the proposed therapy procedures, as well as bureaucratic red-tape which frustrates and complicates any creative approach. Public agencies fear a negative public reaction to hypnosis. (It may well be that the public is too misinformed about the subject to react favourably.)

Another reason for the delay in the widespread use of hypnosis, in fields where it is already known and acknowledged to have beneficial uses, is that we live in such a drug-oriented culture that it is inconceivable to many people that chemically-produced problems can be corrected by non-chemical means. There is another aspect which should be admitted, and that is the fact that there is a fantastic amount of money in the drug business, both legitimate and illegitimate, and somebody would lose a tremendous amount of money if hypnotherapy were widely adopted for these problems.

Lastly, there is a basic reluctance to concentrate on the real personality problems involved. Many people are not looking for a cure, but rather for a substitute 'crutch'. This is especially true in cases of alcohol and drug abuse.

Isn't there a danger of developing a worse symptom if hypnosis is used to remove a symptom?

For many years some writers have popularized the theory that *all* neurotic symptoms have a hidden cause repressed in the unconscious and the symptom therefore fulfils some unknown psychological need. Under such circumstances, if the symptom was merely removed or further repressed it would cause this unfulfilled 'need' to be expressed in another symptom which might be worse than the first one. Thus, according to this theory, if a person stops smoking, he may overeat; if he stops overeating, he may then bite his nails; if the nail-biting symptom is suppressed, he may take to drink, etc. Symptom will follow symptom in rapid succession, growing worse each time until the person could conceivably end in suicide.

The first thing to be said of this theory is that it is strongly challenged by contemporary psychologists, doctors, and behavioural therapists. In an overwhelming percentage of cases it simply does not hold true. Furthermore, if this theory were always true (and it is not), since most modern medical practice deals with symptomatic relief, it would be a far more serious indictment against medical practice than against hypnotic treatment.

In actual practice, few, if any, symptoms can be suppressed by hypnosis without dealing with the underlying causes, anxieties, etc. If direct suggestion (over a period of time) does not remove the symptoms, then hypnosis can be used effectively to search out the underlying causes and deal with them.

Isn't it necessary to get 'insight' to cure psychological problems? Does hypnosis help to get this insight?

Some psychological problems do not seem to clear up until the patient gets an insight into the cause and make-up of the problem. On the other hand, many such problems are successfully treated through the conditioning of behaviour therapies which totally ignore even the possibility of repressed 'causes' in the Freudian sense. Lastly, it is by no means unusual for patients in psychotherapy to get 'insight' without any significant improvement in symptom relief.

Hypnosis is a method that can be compatible with any theory, from Freudian to Pavlovian. It can be helpful to any kind of therapist who deals with any kind of patient.

When 'insight' is essential, it can be achieved by several methods, all of which have at least a partial relationship with hypnological science. Because it deals with the subconscious, hypnoanalysis is recognized as one of the superior techniques in such situations. It can bring the repressed 'cause' from unconsciousness when the patient is unable or unwilling to recall it. This is only one method of hypnotherapy, however, and not always the one chosen. There are many possible causes even for the same kind of symptoms and a personalized approach is always advisable.

Can counsellors, such as guidance counsellors, marriage counsellors, etc., use hypnosis?

The essential quality of rapport and relaxation in the counselling interview can be immensely facilitated by an understanding of hypnological principles, as can the free flow of conversation and creative ideas which make a session successful. Hypnosis (in the conventional sense) can only be used with the consent of the client, but helpful ideas may be suggested indirectly to the client to help him work out his problems.

In each of the caring professions there are several schools of thought regarding correct counselling principles. Basically the issue is whether a counsellor should be directive and tell his client what should be done and persuade him to do it; or whether he should be non-directive, permissive, and merely help the client to clarify his thinking about his goals and values, and then trust the client to follow his own plans to achieve his goals. In actual practice a mixture of both approaches is used in most cases.

Whichever approach is followed, a judicious use of hypnological principles (if not actually hypnosis itself) can be helpful to both the counsellor and the client. Hypnosis should be used only to help people accomplish what they want or need, and never as a coercive technique.

It must be remembered that hypnosis in no way makes the subject unaware or under the influence of the hypnotist. Any suggestion which conflicts with the deepest needs and desires of the hypnotized person is not accepted or acted upon under any conditions or circumstances whatever. The idea that this can happen is a myth which ought to be exposed and dispelled once and for all.

Is hypnosis a form of counselling?

The permissive method of hypnotic induction and the usual type of counselling session have much in common. The essential quality of rapport, mutual confidence, and a willingness to confide are common to both. Both are interpersonal relationships which deal with psychological defence mechanisms and uncover a certain amount of moderately or greatly repressed material in the client's mind. The most successful counsellors intuitively use hypnological methods in modified forms and a more studied and deliberate use of them would no doubt increase counselling success.

It is a very healthy concept of hypnosis to consider it as a form of communication. Because it is a temporarily intimate interpersonal relationship, it carries with it serious ethical consequences for the hypnotist. It is in this context that the so-called 'dangers' of hypnotism are best understood. The 'dangers' of hypnosis are precisely, no more and no less, those of any other interpersonal relationship.

Hypnosis itself goes beyond counselling, however. It is counselling within the context of the hypnotic relationship which involves the existence of the trance and a by-pass of the critical faculties of the client, factors which are not involved in normal counselling.

Of what value is hypnosis in the field of education?

Hypnosis is of value to educators in the same way it can be of value to psychologists: in both experimental and applied ways. Enough hypnotic experimentation in perception and memory has been done to demonstrate its potential usefulness in applied education. Certain findings in hypnotic research, such as the time-distortion phenomenon, could have a revolutionary impact on the learning process. The uniquely new need in rapidly changing technology situations for 'selective forgetting' (where a person may need to 'forget' obsolete information, such as an air traffic controller who must forget old airline patterns in order to remember new ones, etc.) would seem to require serious attention to the potential of hypnosis.

Since teachers and lecturers are faced with such problems as stimulating students to learn, overcoming their mental blocks about certain subjects, rapid learning of increased amounts of material, instilling studious habits, etc., as well as developing situations in which the curriculum can be mastered and creativity fostered, it should be obvious that they cannot afford to ignore the possibilities of scientifically applied hypnosis.

Would it be practical to use hypnosis in the classroom?

For many years teachers have been in the habit of asking students for their 'undivided attention'. The most practical way of achieving this would be by hypnosis. The rare and much sought-after state of relaxed concentration should be taught to every student; only hypnosis can achieve this effect.

Emotional tensions which inhibit learning can make classroom recitations a misery for some children and cause 'test anxiety' which robs students even of the credit they deserve; but such tensions can all be effectively reduced and even eliminated through hypnosis. Of course, it would require teachers especially trained in proper techniques, and various types of 'learning laboratories' would be ideal for educational hypnosis, whether it is called hypnosis or something else.

The major obstacles to implementing such proposals would, of course, be in the parental or community opposition — due to the ignorance of the public concerning the nature, benefits, harmlessness, and utility of hypnosis. There is no real reason why hypnological principles could not be applied effectively with beneficial results in all phases of education, even if some other name were used for them.

Could hypnosis in educational classwork be automated, or mechanically programmed by the use of tape recorders, etc.?

The educational value of tape recorders, videos, closed-circuit television, computers, etc. is well established. Experimental and clinical hypnotists have also proven the feasibility of 'automated hypnosis' with these and other technological aids. There is no reason why students could not be grouped suitably and efficiently helped in this way.

People have great difficulty in seeing the value of intangibles and hypnosis may be ignored simply because it does not require any 'hardware' as such. Educational institutions are not accustomed to paying for programmes which do not have tangible components — they must occupy floor space and involve kickable objects, otherwise they are not worth spending money on. Since no chemicals, drugs, gadgets, or special equipment are necessary in hypnotism, it may be hard for those in education to take it seriously. However, automated hypnosis is practical, and might be the only way that the benefits of hypnosis can ever be 'sold' to education.

Automated techniques of hypnotism still require the guidance of expert hypnotists; otherwise the concept degenerates into a useless science-fiction gadgetry. All the automated equipment in the world does not 'do' anything unless it is directed and supervised by trained personnel.

Can hypnosis be used to motivate students?

Hypnotism is not a method to coerce people into doing what they do not want to do; it is, however, a most effective method of helping people to achieve their goals.

The problem of the unmotivated student is not really a total lack of motivation! Everyone is motivated in some sense; each person has 'motivation'. The problem teachers face is that some students have been 'turned off' regarding school in general or certain subjects in particular; they are selectively unmotivated. The unmotivated student may actually suffer from a crippled self-concept (as a student) and an inability to relate academic tasks to his own goals. Perhaps a deficiency in basic learning skills plus some deeply personal emotional problems may be the cause of his seeming lack of motivation in learning. (Remember, he may have plenty of motivation for other activities, but he is selectively unmotivated regarding at least part of his educational experience.)

When the problems of the unmotivated student are considered in this light, it can be seen immediately how hypnosis could be helpful. Hypnosis is useless in 'motivating' a person if it is used just as another way of telling him what to do when he does not want to do it. However, rightly applied hypnosis can work wonders for the poor student.

Could a student use self-hypnosis?

Yes, and many of the best ones do without knowing it! People who are extremely successful in achievements which require careful attention, extreme concentration, and sustained self-discipline *in whatever field of activity*, usually have stumbled onto some mental techniques which have made them more successful than they otherwise would have been. Upon careful examination, these techniques bear strong resemblance to the methods of self-hypnosis.

A scientific approach to self-hypnosis would make a proven method of success available to all who need it. (And who needs it more than students who are preparing for the future?) Every student, beginning at the first year of schooling, should be taught self-hypnosis as a method of self-involvement in goal-seeking activities. Self-hypnosis is not an escape or an amusement — it is a state of effortless concentration in a self-induced and self-directed state of heightened awareness.

A student can use self-hypnosis to prepare his mind to study for a specified period without fatigue or distraction and to remember clearly what he studies. (Seldom is self-hypnosis used to study in a trance state.) It is used to reduce anxiety under pressure so that the mind can be relaxed and refreshed in recalling material during tests or exams.

What kinds of students would most benefit from hypnosis?

Research that has been done with hypnosis and students indicates that the most dramatic effects are with the 'under-achievers'. In other words, although *all* students benefit to some degree, the degree of improvement is most noticeable, most measurable, and most astounding in those who have the most room for improvement.

(Much of the past research has been with undergraduate psychology students in universities, and little of this was designed to have practical application on a broader basis.)

However, there is every reason to believe that experiments *designed* to stimulate excellent students to learn new subjects faster and more easily would yield positive results. In short, we cannot expect the results to be beyond the purpose of the experiments. All clinical applications on students' problems have reported excellent results.

With a proper sub-grouping of students, in terms of their need and susceptibility, hypnosis can be just as effective in groups as in individual cases. There is reason to expect that the best results would be with younger pupils and some form of hypnological training would be very productive even on the kindergarten level.

Would hypnosis be safe if employed in the schools?

Hypnosis is always safe when employed properly by qualified persons. Anyone using hypnosis should be well-trained and acting within the area of his or her competence. Despite the myths perpetuated by public superstition and ignorance, hypnosis remains one of the safest procedures known and what dangers are involved are well-known and easily avoided.

In view of the fact that hypnosis is a form of communication, based on a temporary intimate interpersonal relationship, the question is the same as asking, 'Is *teaching* safe if employed in the schools?' or, 'Is *counselling* safe if employed in the schools?' etc.

One possible area of concern is that students may attempt to hypnotize each other once they are familiar with the methods. This is unlikely to be successful even if attempted (experience has proven this) and can easily be prevented in one of two ways: by including post-hypnotic suggestions which would prevent unauthorized persons from ever hypnotizing them; or by using such disguised induction techniques that the students do not equate their experience with 'hypnosis'.

Trained hypnotists are qualified to identify possible dangers in its use or misuse. Hypnosis should not be prohibited by uninformed people who worry about totally non-existent problems.

Does hypnosis have a use in law enforcement?

There has been great interest recently in the possible uses of hypnosis in law enforcement. Many barristers and solicitors have taken both a personal and professional interest in the science of hypnosis and are attending seminars on the subject. Since this is a relatively new application of hypnosis, there is some danger that exaggerated claims will be made by over-enthusiastic lay hypnotists and when hypnosis cannot deliver on their wild promises, it may become discredited and totally abandoned.

It must be clearly understood what hypnosis *can* and *cannot* do in law enforcement. It *cannot* be used as an infallible lie-detector and it *cannot* be used to extort confessions. It *can* be used to help witnesses and victims recall details which, when followed up by routine detective work, will yield 'hard' evidence which will be admissible in court. Its primary use will be with police officers, witnesses and victims rather than with criminals or suspects. Although it has been used successfully in this way, it is seldom that actual testimony given under hypnosis is admissible evidence in a trial, which is as it should be.

How could hypnosis be applied in the rehabilitation of criminals and delinquents?

Hypnosis has been proven to be of value in the rehabilitation of juvenile delinquents in published articles by the author ('Hypnotherapeutic Rehabilitation of Juvenile Delinquents', 'Juvenile Delinquency and Hypnosis', and 'Delinquent and Criminal Rehabilitation') and others. There are also indications that it could be successful in the rehabilitation of certain types of criminals.

In dealing with the psychological problems often found in criminals and delinquents, hypnosis can always be a helpful adjunct to other forms of psychotherapy. However, the author's wide experience in the field of corrections has led him to the firm conclusion that hypnotherapy should be the *definitive* and preferred treatment in such cases!

Again it must be emphasized that hypnosis is not a coercive form of treatment, nor a simple short-cut to a utopian reform of criminals. It is a method to make more effective and efficient the other methods of casework, counselling and psychotherapy.

Hypnosis could be a part of the treatment process involving criminals or delinquents at any point of probation, confinement or parole. As a medical adjunct, it could apply to nearly every type of patient found in prison hospitals as well as in specific therapeutic efforts with selected inmates.

If delinquents and criminals in institutions could be reformed by hypnosis, would this be a violation of their civil rights?

The simplest way to solve the problems of 'rights' of institutionalized persons is to make all 'treatment' purely voluntary. (As opposed to the custodial functions.) Hypnosis is a 'consent state' and should only be attempted with people who voluntarily consent to it.

To many people the concept that hypnosis can 'reform' criminals is a vaguely threatening one, calling up a combination of Gestapo and Frankenstein-ish images to their minds. However, it should be apparent that we are speaking of hypno*therapy* and before it will actually be used on any large scale in this area, there will have to be some changes in prison management.

If more qualified persons could be induced to work in prisons, such settings could become invaluable laboratories in which to advance our knowledge of human behaviour and sociopathology. Prisons would be ideal places in which to use scientific hypnosis in voluntary experiments on a variety of vital social and medical problems. The structured environment would also make possible, and extremely feasible, the use of automated, programmed techniques of hypnotherapy.

Would delinquents and criminals ever really consent to hypnotherapy?

The advantage of gaining a delinquent's consent for hypnotherapy over other therapies has been dealt with in the author's 'Hypnotherapeutic Rehabilitation of Juvenile Delinquents', (presented at the Panamerican Medical Convention in Buenos Aires in 1967). There are aspects of hypnotherapy which actually make it easier to enlist the co-operation of patients than is true in conventional therapies.

Even with so-called sociopaths or psychopaths, there are often certain areas of their lives which they will consent to have treated and these peripheral matters may play an important part in opening them up to more vital aspects of the therapeutic process. Even the most ignorant, depraved or disgusting persons in the world have something they would like help with; and the permissive, non-threatening types of hypnosis can establish rapport with this kind of person and can lead to more comprehensive treatment.

It is the author's opinion that the persons trained to use hypnosis in corrective institutions should be recruited from personnel such as probation or parole officers, etc., rather than psychologists, social workers, and so on, imported from the outside. Much of the failure of psychotherapy with criminals seems due to the not altogether unjustified inability of the inmate to relate to a 'headshrinker'.

Are there military uses of hypnosis?

Because of its involvement in education, instruction, training and medical treatment of personnel, the armed forces can make the same use of hypnosis as can teachers, psychologists and medical doctors. Because of the inherent security functions and organizational apparatus of the military, some possible uses of hypnosis are the same as in civilian law enforcement agencies.

There have been many fanciful and mostly fictional hints that hypnosis has been used in the field of espionage and counter-espionage. The possible uses of hypnotic training for perfect recall, amnesia-block for coded messages transmitted by couriers, automatic responses to post-hypnotic suggestions, resistance to torture and interrogation techniques, etc., have been researched and used in limited ways. It must be understood that the 'other side' has perfectly competent hypnotists as well and most of the hypnotic applications in 'spy stuff' is best left to fiction writers.

Some instruction in methods of self-hypnosis for the control of pain, resistance to fatigue, climate, and so on, is of practical value in all forms of 'survival training' for military personnel, and should be widely used.

Couldn't businessmen, salesmen, etc., use the principles of hypnotism in the business world?

Hypnotists knowingly use 'sales psychology', but those who teach salesmanship are often ignorant of their debt to hypnological science. Individual salesmen are always looking for ways to motivate themselves and many have found that self-hypnotic methods are the most effective. All business people who are basically self-directed and self-motivated have also found self-hypnosis to be of great practical help.

The advertising business and media industry are intensely interested in all aspects of psychology which pertain to sales and marketing. The more subtle forms of persuasion (the 'image making' and the task of public relations in business and politics) all incorporate some aspect of hypnology. The challenging possibilities of subliminal communication (messages which are perceived subconsciously, because they are transmitted faster than the eye or ear, can normally distinguish consciously) are directly related to hypnological science, which also conducts research in this area.

If hypnosis is conceived of as a method to manipulate behaviour through unconsciously perceived messages and motivations, then business would obviously be interested in it. Through mass media methods the hypnotic techniques which have been developed for person-to-person use could be used on a company (or government)-to-public basis. This Orwellian prospect is uncomfortably possible and all too probable.

How could the individual businessman, executive or salesman benefit from hypnosis?

The benefits of hypnosis and self-hypnosis are especially pertinent to the needs of people in business and sales. Personal requirements and job demands combine to give them certain problems which can best be dealt with by scientific hypnosis.

The built-in stress of the competitive business world causes many executives to try and cope with it in destructive ways, such as the alcohol-and-tranquillizer routine. The ability to control one's emotional states, to work with a relaxed intensity, and to think clearly without being handicapped by temporary emotional problems, is most easily acquired through training in self-hypnosis. The benefits are obvious to the executive.

Single-mindedness of purpose, disciplined motivation toward goals, deadlines and quotas, the ability to drive oneself independently of supervision, etc., are of supreme advantage to all salesmen and businesspersons. These qualities cannot be obtained from taking a pill, but only from some form of mental discipline; self-hypnosis is the only practical way to do it. The relaxation and confidence which are the by-products of habitual self-hypnosis would increase the efficiency and success of anyone in the business world.

What is the connection between religion and hypnosis?

Some people might find any 'connection' between religion and hypnosis objectionable. This attitude is understandable in view of the historical development of hypnotism and current public misinformation. Hypnosis can 'explain' some strange phenomena remotely related to religion, but it cannot explain everything and it most certainly does not 'explain away' anything in religion.

Both hypnology and religion deal with human psychology and the subconscious mind in particular. To that extent, there is a natural connection between them. Furthermore, both fields afford examples of uncommon and extreme behavioural manifestations which defy ordinary analysis. Hypnosis is a natural phenomenon and a science; it should not be treated as if it were occult or quasi-religious in nature. Like any science, it sometimes contributes to religious thought, and sometimes (temporarily) seems to threaten it. Truth does not contradict itself, so if scientific truth and moral truth sometimes 'connect', neither is made poorer and both can be enriched.

The many ramifications of the 'connection' between hypnosis and religion have been dealt with in the section on 'Spiritual Improvement' in the author's book, *Self-Improvement Through Self-Hypnosis.*

Are the churches for or against hypnosis?

Throughout history, hypnotism has frequently travelled in bad company. Until it was divested of its superstitious mystique by scientific study, hypnotism was often used by witch-doctors, sorcerers, etc., to distort and obscure the truth. Because of its misuse and apparent connection with pagan beliefs and practices, it was quite proper for the Church in previous centuries to reject and condemn that type of hypnotism.

As truth conquered error, knowledge overcame ignorance, and science replaced superstition, hypnotism 'came clean' and the Church recognized this totally new situation. The Roman Catholic Church began its *official* study into hypnosis, as a method for painless childbirth, and subsequently endorsed its medical and ethical uses by a declaration of Pope Pius XII. Since then a number of theologians have studied the moral and religious aspects of hypnosis and have unanimously declared it to be amoral rather than immoral, and perfectly moral when used for moral ends.

A few Protestant denominations officially oppose the use of hypnosis, but this is merely a reflection of their general anti-scientific orientation. (Hypnosis is officially condemned only by the Jehovah's Witnesses and the Christian Science Church.) Because they are uninformed, a few church groups are rather suspicious of hypnosis but take no official stand one way or the other.

Do ministers sometimes have a hypnotic control over their people?

Yes, but only in the sense that some teachers and salesmen have a 'hypnotic' control over the people they deal with. This is a metaphorical way of speaking, not a scientific way. Whenever a person has a personal magnetism and persuasiveness to the point where he has a following, it is common to speak of his influence as 'hypnotic'. However, hypnotism involves a by-pass of the critical faculty, trance, and suggestion; only when these elements are present should personal influence be called 'hypnotic'.

There sometimes occur situations in religious gatherings where all the necessary elements are present to designate it as hypnotic; in such situations, the minister is as 'hypnotized' as the congregation. Ritual and formalized situations can take the place of a hypnotist under certain circumstances. (See the author's book, *Self-Improvement Through Self-Hypnosis*.) In this way, some 'religious' phenomena can also be considered 'hypnotic', but the minister's role in it is usually minimal.

Clergymen point out that if God does not exercise hypnotic control over people, why should they? They will also privately lament that the non-religious person's concept of the 'control' they have over their flock is grossly exaggerated!

Could clergymen use hypnosis to advantage?

It is the considered opinion of the author that anyone could use hypnosis to advantage; clergymen are no exception. Indeed, a clergyman has a special need to understand the science of hypnosis.

The emotional and psychological demands on a conscientious clergyman are tremendous. He is expected to minister to all kinds of people who are usually angry, frightened, confused, bereaved, worried, etc., and still maintain his personal calm and emotional balance at all times. He fills the role of an executive in planning and administering church business, and that of a salesman of ideas, ideals, and programmes to his congregation and to the community. On top of all that, he must study, pray and maintain his own spiritual life at a level above his parishioners.

To understand better the subconscious mind and the strange mind-body phenomena of the trance, the clergyman could benefit from a scientific understanding of hypnosis. In disguised forms suitable to his role, a minister can use such knowledge to help people who are trying to cope with the problems of life. A scientific grasp of hypnosis and suggestion will help him to evaluate properly certain phenomena which otherwise might be mis-labelled as 'spiritual' or 'religious'. A clergyman could very well use hypnosis with advantage to his ministry, his congregation, and himself.

Could the average religious person utilize self-hypnosis to advantage?

It should be easy to understand how a religious person (like any other) could use self-hypnosis to advantage, for a religious person is not exempt from emotional stress.

The real question is whether self-hypnosis could be used to advantage in a person's *religious* life. The answer is that self-hypnosis is a short-cut to meditative attitudes and awareness; in that sense it is of great value to a religious person. What otherwise would only be discovered accidentally (if at all) after long, and perhaps fruitless, practice can be learned in a few minutes with a competent instructor in self-hypnosis. The mental stillness and calm concentration so helpful in prayer can be rapidly developed through self-hypnosis.

Another benefit of a religious person's study of self-hypnosis is that it should enable him or her to distinguish between natural or psychological states and those which may be supernatural or spiritual in nature. Many would-be saints were misled by their psychologically-induced visions and sensations; great saints were sceptical of phenomena which they suspected might be purely hypnotic in nature. A spiritual person, with a scientific orientation about hypnosis, is in a unique position to evaluate properly his or her inner experiences.

Is there a relationship between hypnosis and yoga?

Yoga is actually a philosophy of life which encompasses many differing schools of thought and practice. The most popular form is hatha yoga, which involves the various postures which have become identified with yoga.

The aim of yoga is 'union' with a Higher Power and harmony with oneself. Various disciplines involving certain postures, breathing exercises and meditation, have evolved over the centuries to accomplish this. Scientific hypnotists have studied the various states of awareness and mind-body feats associated with yoga and have evaluated them from a hypnological point of view. It is generally agreed that many yoga practices are variations of common self-hypnosis techniques, and the resulting mental state is the same as in self-hypnosis.

It is alleged that the more spectacular feats of the yogis require a sort of super-trance called 'samadhi'. Recent investigations seem to indicate that 'samadhi' is the equivalent of hypnotic trance, usually of the 'ergotropic' type. It is also doubtful whether 'samadhi' is actually essential as a prerequisite to perform the spectacular feats of yoga.

What is the connection, if any, between 'transcendental meditation' and 'self-hypnosis'?

When many drug-oriented young people turned to oriental philosophy some years ago, in search for new and meaningful experiences, many took up the practice of meditation as an alternative to mind-expanding drugs. 'Transcendental meditation' became a passing fad with many, but a continuing and helpful practice for others.

Meditation is a way of using the mind; it is a method for achieving calm undistracted attention which is analogous, if not identical, to self-hypnosis. Self-hypnosis is a form of meditation and meditation is a form of self-hypnosis. Self-hypnosis is a scientific way of achieving the desired mental state quickly and consistently.

There is nothing particularly 'transcendental' about this method of meditation, any more than self-hypnosis can be considered a 'mystical' or 'religious' experience. Only when the *object* of one's meditation is of a transcendental or spiritual quality should it be referred to in those terms. Those who are interested in meditation for spiritual self-improvement will find that self-hypnosis will help them attain the state of awareness and undivided attention which will best suit their purpose, without unnecessary and time-consuming rituals.

Could hypnosis be considered 'mind-expanding' or 'psychedelic'?

The term 'psychedelic' was coined to describe the hallucinatory drug-induced experience in a more positive way. In the early days of research with LSD and similar chemicals, the experience which resulted from taking them was called 'psychotomimetic' because it seemed to duplicate the psychotic illness of schizophrenia. In other words, the results of the drugs imitated mental illness, and there were initial enthusiastic hopes that the chemicals could be helpful in research on schizophrenia.

Soon an LSD 'cult' developed which believed that it was a sort of short-cut to cosmic consciousness and a method of spiritual and mystical attainment. To avoid the negative connotation of labelling the experience as merely imitative of insanity (as the term 'psychotomimetic' did), the term 'psychedelic' or 'mind manifesting' was coined instead. Soon both the drugs and the experiences they produced were called 'mind-expanding'. These terms have no precise scientific meaning. They sound wholesome and intriguing, but they ignore and trivialize known dangers and the negative aspects of 'bad trips'. In what sense the 'mind' is 'expanded' is unclear.

After hypnotism was used to study hysteria in the 1880s, it soon developed into a safe, respected method for research and treatment. It deserves to be called 'mind-expanding' in the most positive sense.

Are drugs ever used in hypnotizing people?

In the years during and subsequent to World War II there was a great deal of work done in combining the effects of drugs and hypnosis. Specialized therapies known as 'narco-hypnosis', 'narco-analysis' and 'narco-synthesis' were attempted in military psychiatric hospitals.

The hope was that drugs could overcome resistance to hypnosis, facilitate the hypnotic induction, and ensure a better and more workable trance. This did not prove to be true. In general, it was found that drugs obscure rather than clarify the hypnotic process. The individual patient's sensitivity to the drugs was so varied that the procedure required too much specialized medical expertise to make it practical. Even when the procedure was relatively successful, the results were not uniformly satisfactory.

The desire for a hypnotic drug, a 'magic potion', etc., is always an indication of incompetence in hypnotic induction. Induction methods have been refined until at present there is very little interest in the use of drugs to induce hypnosis; there is really no need for such drugs. Some mildly tranquillizing drugs have helped some patients, but even in those cases it is really unnecessary. Drugs do not help in inducing hypnosis in refractory subjects, and are not needed for willing subjects.

What other groups of people might use hypnosis in their work?

There is hardly any group which could not find hypnosis or self-hypnosis of some value, either in terms of their individual personal lives or in ways directly relating to their work.

Athletes have found hypnosis of great help when properly used. Some humorous or foolish examples have sometimes been reported in the press, but the fact remains that many athletes have been helped through hypnosis. Again, when hypnosis is expected to work instant miracles, it is always a disappointment, but when it is judiciously applied as part of an overall programme, it gives encouraging results. All athletes know the importance of getting 'psyched up' before a competition, but few realize the importance of cultivating a 'winner's attitude' every day in practice or competition. Solitary athletes can use hypnosis to overcome the mental block in breaking a long-standing 'record' as well as for their personal motivation and training discipline.

Show business people, mainly performers, have found hypnosis helpful in memorizing their lines, overcoming the 'jitters', and visualizing the proper performance. Many 'troupers' use self-hypnosis to help them rest better, learn better and perform better. Of course, the creative behind-the-scenes people can also use hypnological principles in less spectacular but perhaps even more important ways.

How can hypnosis be specifically used in athletics?

The psychological training of the athlete is just as important as the physical training; the desire and discipline for physical training is a result of the psychological training.

The many mind-over-body aspects of athletics, such as resistance to pain and fatigue, have an obvious relationship with hypnosis. The team athlete has the stimulus and encouragement of the cheering crowd as well as his coach and team-mates to help him achieve this, but the solitary athlete must rely on his personal inner resources for this extra help. The long-distance runner or swimmer, the golfer, the tennis player, the field athlete, etc., must get 'psyched up', and self-hypnosis is ideal for them.

A sports record usually stands for a long time but, once it is broken, the new record is frequently bettered by other athletes soon after. Then the suggestion of the 'unbeatable' record takes effect and that record stands until someone else breaks the new psychological barrier of imagined 'impossibility'. By 'time-projection' through hypnosis, the athlete can see himself in the future and re-orient himself to the 'new' records which exist then. This subconscious certainty that records can and will be broken can be of great value in motivating the athlete for more disciplined practice and performance.

Is hypnosis in athletics legitimate and ethical?

To some people the use of hypnosis in athletics seems like a form of cheating comparable to 'doping' horses in a race. The common contemporary use of pain-killers, stimulants, inhalants, 'special diets', hormone injections, etc., make such an objection naïvely irrelevant. There are many dubious practices in athletics today and the use of hypnosis would be a breath of fresh air by comparison.

Such an objection also shows a total misunderstanding of the nature and possibilities of hypnosis. To use the mind *in a perfectly natural way* to extend one's normal capabilities for increased physical and mental achievement is certainly legitimate by any standards. Incorporated into the total training programme under the watchful supervision of coaches, trainers, and doctors, hypnosis would be the least harmful and most hopeful of many methods currently in use. An athlete's personal problems can have an adverse effect on his sports performance and hypnotherapy by a qualified person would help the athlete *as an athlete* also.

Hypnosis is a science. Most coaches and trainers, and their athletes, would probably resort to the use of voodoo dolls if they thought it would help them win!

Do many people in show business use self-hypnosis?

Many *successful* people, including those in the entertainment business, use self-hypnosis in a haphazard way without knowing it. Some use it scientifically and they literally consider it to be a 'secret' of their success.

The confidence and positive mental attitude required to audition, rehearse and perform against professional competition, public reaction, and critical review is considerable. The entertainer must maintain a proper frame of mind towards his work in spite of personal problems; this is the kind of help that self-hypnosis can give. The task of memorizing new parts, visualizing them, 'getting into' the part and projecting the performance, *then forgetting the whole thing* and doing the same with an altogether different role, requires a unique mental ability. Top professionals utilize every tool and trick of the trade; hypnosis is one of the tools available.

Performers such as dancers have the same needs, as do successful athletes, and self-hypnosis can help them in the same ways. Again, professional entertainers are disciplined people who compete to stay employed, and use every possible help to get and stay at the top. Many show business people are superstitious, but the best ones use hypnosis scientifically.

What about applications of hypnosis in the non-performing, creative arts?

Artists, sculptors, authors, playwrights, composers, etc., have temperamental traits and work demands in common which can benefit greatly from hypnosis and self-hypnosis. Creative people (whether self-employed or not) must be able to work for intense periods in relative solitude and sustain themselves by their own introspective processes. They must cultivate the subconscious side of their lives and be more 'conscious of the subconscious', so to speak, for they must draw upon this side of their nature to do creative work. Self-hypnosis facilitates this ability and places it under voluntary control.

Although often considered 'arty' and erratic, such people must be able to motivate themselves and work long hours under self-imposed deadlines in order to be successful and creatively fulfilled. They are susceptible to extremes of emotion and must have strong confidence in what they are doing in order to survive abnormally vivid periods of discouragement.

Hypnosis and self-hypnosis enable a person to have a voluntary control over emotional states and thereby maintain a more even quality and productivity in the creative arts.

Can hypnosis stimulate creativity?

Studies of creative people indicate that they have a natural aptitude to use their minds, in ways that ordinary people only experience on rare occasions, in what could be broadly defined as a hypnotic state. An essential part of 'creativity' is the ability to utilize all the senses in perceiving and 'visualizing', to see unusual relationships and unique applications of commonplace things, and to 'tap' the subconscious mind to enhance that ability.

Although creativity is difficult to define and complex to study, all available research indicates that everyone could be taught to be more creative. It would seem logical that hypnosis (with its ability to establish a two-way communication with the subconscious mind) could play a vital part in teaching people to use their minds in more creative ways. Analysis of the lives and writings of creative people indicates that they habitually (although usually unconsciously) used hypnological principles to stimulate the flow of their creative ideas, and to motivate themselves successfully to achieve the embodiment of those ideas.

The hypnotic stimulation of creativity will undoubtedly become a fruitful area for research and application in the future.

Can the 'subconscious' be defined?

The idea of a 'subconscious' mind is nothing new. Even in ancient writings, great thinkers seem to have recognized a dual construction of the human mind. It has always been apparent that much of man's ideas and behaviour spring from sources of which he is not normally aware. Thus, 'subconscious' merely refers to that part of human thinking processes which go on below the level of conscious awareness.

Freud focused attention on the importance of unconscious processes, and wrote of the conscious, the pre-conscious and the unconscious. Much of what modern hypnologists refer to as the 'subconscious' would equate with what Freud called the 'pre-conscious' mind. Although some writers object to the term 'subconscious', because they feel the prefix 'sub' implies inferiority, the term has gained steadily in popularity since it was first coined by Pierre Janet.

For many, the 'subconscious' became synonymous with older metaphysical concepts of 'soul', etc. This is unnecessary and rather non-productive. Since hypnosis is now understood in a neurological and psychophysiological frame of reference, perhaps the simplest and most scientific definition would be that the subconscious mind is the sum total of all neurological and biochemical functions of the organism which take place below the level of consciousness.

How does hypnosis affect the subconscious?

The apparatus of the subconscious mind is the nervous system, which is stimulated in certain ways during hypnotic induction to produce a trance. The trance may be conceived as the result of stimulation of either the sympathetic or parasympathetic nervous system, as explained in Chapter 3.

In practical everyday terms, hypnosis opens up a channel of communication with the subconscious mind. To use the computer analogy, hypnosis establishes an 'input' and an 'output' capacity between the conscious and the subconscious mind. Hidden or forgotten material in the subconscious can be retrieved and desirable material can be 'programmed' into it for future use, to mobilize the person's resources toward definite and predetermined aims.

Although this cybernetic, materialistic way of thinking about the subconscious may offend those who confuse it and hypnosis with metaphysical concepts, it is the simplest way to explain to most people the nature of the subconscious, and the extremely practical applications of the science of hypnosis in affecting it.

Are there laws restricting the use of hypnosis?

In many communities there are still remnants of certain restrictive laws which are fifty years out-of-date. These ordinances, known as 'gypsy laws', were meant to keep undesirables out of the community, and sometimes specify 'fortune-tellers, clairvoyants, *hypnotists*'! Such antiquated laws are sometimes used to discriminate against non-medical hypnotists, regardless of their educational or professional qualifications. If enforced uniformly, they could also restrict medical hypnotists and scientific investigators; of course, they are not impartially enforced.

The constitutionality of these laws is doubtful and if they were tested by court cases would probably be repealed. Certainly any citizen ought to have a civil right to pursue any kind of knowledge, including hypnosis, or to avail himself of the benefits of hypnosis, if he so chooses.

How can the average, everyday person benefit from hypnosis?

First of all, by knowing the *power* inherent in one's own mind. A study of hypnosis calls dramatic attention to the powers that are both latent and at work in the mind of every person. The first benefit that a student of hypnosis receives is the awareness that this amazing power actually resides within his or her own mind! To realize that extraordinary power resides within all ordinary people is a revolutionary thought for most people.

Secondly, the study of hypnosis quickly leads one to an awareness of the *possibility* of changing, directing, and in general using his subconscious powers for a better life. The study of hypnosis reveals the accessibility of the subconscious and its susceptibility to change, modification and re-direction.

Thirdly, the study of hypnosis presents a method by which a practical and effective *programme* of self-improvement can be devised and followed.

Every person, no matter how 'average' or 'everyday', wants to be better in some aspect of life. Hypnosis and self-hypnosis can help a person to become what he wants to be and achieve what he wants to do.

Isn't it dangerous for the average person to tamper with the subconscious?

One's subconscious mind is continually being 'tampered with' throughout one's lifetime. From birth onward, the subconscious is functioning and 'doing its thing'. It absorbs every word, thought, and experience of one's life. Every person, place, and thing in one's life affects the subconscious. Every book, article, film, television programme and advertisement — as well as each comment, criticism and statement — is *indelibly* impressed upon and stored within one's subconscious. This is a never-ending process from birth to death.

Under certain circumstances, the subconscious becomes even more vulnerable to outside influences. These times happen by pure accident, without plan, and therefore are completely unpreventable. (See Chapter 1.) Hypnosis is therefore merely one of the many ways in which one's subconscious is influenced. However, hypnosis is the only scientific way that it can be done in a controlled, purposeful manner. Self-hypnosis puts this scientific ability under the voluntary and intelligent control of the person directly involved.

Shouldn't hypnotic know-how be limited to only a few highly-trained professional people?

There are some who feel that knowledge of hypnosis represents a 'power' that could be misused. In general, it can be stated that such fears are groundless. (See Chapter 4.)

In a sense, hypnotic know-how *is* limited to only a few highly-trained professional people at the present time. Because it is limited to so few, there are millions of people who are deprived of the benefits of hypnosis and significant research proceeds with frustrating slowness. The tiny percentage of medical people who have any hypnotic expertise cannot even handle the cases within their own practices which would benefit from hypnosis, much less be of help in accepting referrals from other doctors. If the number of medical hypnotists were increased a thousand-fold, there *still* would *not* be enough practitioners to utilize hypnosis in all of its medical and non-medical applications.

Attempts to restrict the use of hypnosis to any specific professional group has resulted in less hypnosis being used. The idea that only an élite group should have this knowledge has always resulted in either outright repression of this valuable science or an encouragement to outright charlatanism. Knowledge should be available to all people who are motivated to attain it!

Should there be more laws, or stricter ones, governing the use of hypnosis?

When one realizes the true nature of hypnosis, it is difficult to see how its use could be restricted or governed by law without at the same time equally affecting those areas of education, religion and business which use hypnological principles. Those who would advocate stricter laws, specifically directed against the use or abuse of hypnosis, are misguided and will create the problems they hope to avoid.

There are already satisfactory laws against false advertising, fraud, criminal negligence, practising medicine without being qualified, etc. Any conceivable abuse of hypnosis could be prosecuted successfully under any of these existing laws. Even the much-advocated laws restricting stage and entertainment hypnotism are unnecessary. Instead of creating false fears about hypnotism (and thereby serving the interests of superstition rather than science) it should be sufficient to prosecute under negligence laws *if and when* any harm would come from stage hypnotism, just as one could sue an establishment if one trips over a rug!

Restrictive laws which are unnecessary both from a legal and scientific standpoint serve no purpose, except the selfish ones of those who wish to monopolize and exploit something which could and should be available to all.

Do you think that *everyone* should know how to hypnotize others, and that *everybody* should be hypnotized?

In a world where mass media make possible political, governmental or commercial exploitation and manipulation of the public, through the hypnological principles of subliminal control and scientific suggestion, it may well be that a knowledge of hypnological science is essential for an individual to preserve his or her psychological integrity.

Hypnosis is merely a method to use the mind in a certain way. Because it is based upon the consent and rapport of all interpersonal relationships, it is unlikely that the 'wrong people' will hypnotize anyone. The point is simply this: should everyone be taught to read? Or think? Or communicate? Or pray?

The answer is simple: yes, everyone who wants to! In the closing decades of the twentieth century, it is inconceivable that anyone should advocate anything less than the liberty of the individual to seek, attain and apply knowledge. It is a crime against the rationality of mankind to suppress or distort *in any way* knowledge which could be of incalculable benefit to present and future generations.

Do available books on hypnosis provide reliable information?

Hypnotism is presently enjoying a revival of public interest. Some of this enthusiasm reflects a steady increase of interest in the scientific aspects of psychology; some of it is just part of a current fad.

Popular books are supplied to meet the popular demands. Therefore, some books on hypnotism are written from an occult viewpoint by people who do little more than compile bizarre episodes and exaggerated claims. Lacking a scientific orientation, these books do not contribute any real knowledge of hypnosis. They mislead the would-be student of true hypnotism.

Scientifically-oriented books are supplied to meet a specialized demand. There are fewer of them and they are more expensive and harder to find, but they are authoritative. Many good books on scientific hypnotism are available in the English language. It is a sad fact that one must read a great deal about hypnosis to gain a little solid knowledge and to be able to evaluate the new material which is constantly being published.

How can a person become a hypnotist?

To become anything, a person must study and learn the principles and procedures involved, master specific techniques, and practise assiduously — preferably under expert supervision. Hypnotism can be learned. A superficial knowledge can be gained in a brief time; an entire lifetime is not sufficient to learn all there is to know about it. The science of hypnology is interrelated with many other subjects in the sciences and the humanities.

Basically, one learns to become a hypnotist from someone who is a hypnotist. There is much that can be learned only from personal instruction; many things which are obscure in print become crystal clear in personal conversation with a knowledgeable person. In a secondary sense, all hypnotists are self-taught. They constantly add to their knowledge by study and observation, and refine their techniques through experience.

It takes time to become a good hypnotist. 'Crash courses' make it appear deceptively easy, but much experience with many subjects is essential for real expertise. To *apply* hypnosis ethically in experimental, clinical, or other specialized areas requires a qualified background in those fields, or strict supervision by a qualified person.

Index